RESOLVING DISPUTES IN CHRISTIAN GROUPS

MARLIN E. THOMAS

Windflower
Communications
Winnipeg, Manitoba, Canada

6 - 28 - 02

RESOLVING DISPUTES IN CHRISTIAN GROUPS
Copyright ©1994 Marlin Thomas

Published by Windflower Communications, Winnipeg, MB

Canadian Cataloguing in Publication Data

Thomas, Marlin E.
    Resolving disputes in Christian groups
    Includes bibliographical references and index.
    ISBN 1-895308-15-1

1. Conflict management – Religious aspects – Christian. 2. Group relations training – Religious aspects – Christian. 3. Interpersonal relations – Religious aspects – Christian. I. Title.

HM134.T46 1994   302.3'4   C94-920212-6

Printed by Derksen Printers, Steinbach, MB
Cover Art and Illustrations by Cliff Derksen, Winnipeg, MB

International Standard Book Number: 1-895308-15-1

RESOLVING DISPUTES IN CHRISTIAN GROUPS

ILLUSTRATIONS/FIGURES

To
all those people
who patiently helped me
understand conflict
and to those
who seek to convert
destructive conflict
into an opportunity
for growth.

INTRODUCTION

This is a dangerous book to read.

It is dangerous because if you are a people person it can either anger you or bore you. In your love for people it also can leave you vulnerable to surprise attacks.

It is dangerous because if you are an analytical, logical person it can lead you even farther away from compassion for people. It also can cause you to do greater damage to others.

That does not mean you should put the book aside. Two types of people who should read this book. One type is the person who has no conflict and the other type is the person who is so wrapped up in conflict that vision is impaired.

If you do not have a conflict now, you will have one some day, and you will get through it better if you know how to deal with it. If you are facing a conflict now, you need to be delivered from it. This book can help you.

You must bring together two things if this book is to fulfill its true purpose for you. First, you must never forget that people are always genuinely themselves. People are always people. They may be enigmatic; they may appear to be false; they may be contrary and truly be a pain to you, but they are simply being who they are at that point in time. Second, you must always remember that human behavior is never purely logical or emotional; it is never purely accidental or only "programmed" by a higher power. Human behavior comes out of life. Sometimes it is reactive; other times it is proactive. Sometimes it is planned, but most often it just happens. Because it often just happens, it can be studied, analyzed, and charted by a "systems" approach.

This book seeks to interact with "people as they are" and "people as life has caused them to be." In both cases there is always a physical, social, emotional and spiritual or religious dimension. If you ever lose sight of people as persons you will victimize them. If you fail to see the cycles and the system within which they live, you will never be able to help them find full and lasting deliverance.

You cannot take one passage, section or chapter of this book and declare that "here is the answer" to any problem, or "this fits _____ to a T." When that temptation occurs, read on. You will soon find your theory complicated by another facet of life, personality, or relationship.

I hope that by the time you finish this book, you will understand just a bit better what makes people react and relate the way they do. I hope you also will know enough about how to apply your skills in conflict management so that life may be more comfortable for you and those around you.

I truly hope you never stop searching or learning. This book by no means contains any final answers. At best, it only points in certain directions. As you read, and when you lay it down, do not fail to pray that God will continue to guide you in understanding more fully his complex creation. Do not cease to pray that God will give you more grace as you deal with all kinds of people, all of them his creation, and seek to life your life in a more Christian way.

I cannot begin to recount all those persons who have been invaluable in bringing me to the point of this writing. Willard Claassen's wonderful little book, *Learning to Lead*, first introduced me to the concept of seeking consensus in group decision making. Many other authors also have been my teachers during this pilgrimage. Norman Shawchuck and David Carlson both mentored me through a difficult time in dealing with conflicts in my own life.

The people of two wonderful congregations were my friends as many concepts in this book were researched and then tried out for effectiveness. My family graciously gave me time to write, and a colleague in ministry, Roland Reimer, gave me valuable encouragement and insights. My secretary, Jeannette Dunn, patiently read the first draft and made valuable suggestions from a lay person's point of view. I also want to thank Gilbert Brandt, my publisher and friend, for making this work possible. While many have contributed to this book, I accept all the responsibility for its flaws. My prayer is that by any means many of God's wonderful people will find a light at the end of their long tunnel of conflict and emerge into the wonder of daylight dancing in the meadow of their life.

One of the troublesome aspects of any work is that it is never completed. More material keeps coming to me. I hope that will be a true experience for the readers, also. Life never stops moving forward but continues to grow. May you grow too as Christ leads you onward toward greater maturity in your relationships with others.

Marlin E. Thomas

PART ONE

THEORY:
HOW CONFLICT WORKS

CHAPTER ONE

Resolving Disputes in Christian Groups: An Introduction

What causes fights and quarrels among you? Don't they come from your desires that battle within you? You want something but don't get it. You kill [human spirits] and covet [power], but you cannot have what you want. You quarrel and fight. You do not have, because you do not ask God. When you ask, you do not receive, because you ask with wrong motives, that you may [consume] what you get on your own [desires] (James 4:1-3).

These are the words of the brother of Jesus, the ruling elder in the Jerusalem church, in about A.D. 45. The church was barely fifteen years old.

Did he speak mainly of the church as an organization, or did he speak of individual people who were members of churches? It really does not matter much. Whether individually or corporately, humans have always been more prone to destroy than to redeem if it suited their purposes. Conflict has been around as long as the human race has existed on the face of the earth.

Now, as then, conflict is not easy to deal with. It is often very hard to control. It more easily consumes and destroys than it saves and reconstructs.

Contrary to what James seems to imply, conflict is not always negative or bad. Conflict occurs whenever two or more persons have different points of view on any matter. That in itself is *not* bad. The badness, the sin, the evil comes in doing wrong things to resolve the conflict.

Sometimes our differences can be worked out with little difficulty. Other times they can end a relationship and even lead to sickness and physical death. Sometimes a healthy, vigorous debate at a church meeting can clear the air and resolve difficult issues. Other times it can polarize and even split a church body.

Sometimes attempts to enhance the operations of a Christian organization can vastly expand its ministry. Other times they can devastate and destroy many faithful workers.

One person captured the anguish of such conflict well when

3

she said, "How can so many nice people do so many bad things to each other?"

This book is an attempt to help Christian people learn how to deal with conflict in their church or Christian group in a healthy manner. We must point out at the outset, however, that not all conflicts will be managed correctly. None of us is God. No one in this life will ever resolve all his/her conflicts adequately, for we all partake of the weakness and sin of the human condition. However, that does not mean we should not try.

James continues by saying in 4:7-10, *Submit yourselves, then to God. Resist the devil and he will flee from you. Come near to God and he will come near to you. Wash your hands, you [Christian] sinners and purify your hearts, you double-minded. Grieve, mourn and wail. Change your laughter to mourning and your joy to gloom. Humble yourselves before the Lord and he will lift you up.*

So, instead of enduring conflict after conflict in our Christian environments, we have an obligation to learn more about how to manage them correctly. Knowing is often half the battle. Being able to spot a storm as it begins to arise on the horizon and take immediate protective action is much better than waiting until it is upon us. Knowing how to take protective action in a conflict is also much better than holding our breath and hoping that God will miraculously intervene. He will help, to be sure, but he can help much better when we use the faculties he has given us.

Conflict Resolution in Churches and Christian Groups

During my early years in ministry I once recommended to a church board that the church make a twenty-five dollar annual contribution to a very worthy cause. The first response was, "We've never done it before. Why start now?"

A library committee once asked a church board to underwrite a new library book building proposal costing from $25.00 to $100.00 per year. The argument that almost defeated the request was that no board members had ever checked out any library books.

A Sunday school leader once told me they were thinking about grooming a certain couple for Sunday school leadership. My first inward response was, "Oh no, not them. They're too shy."

These three true stories illustrate what Shad Helmstetter noted so eloquently in a 1987 issue of Family Concern, a church bulletin insert from *Christianity Today*. In a quotation entitled "The Big No," Helmstetter said that as much as 77% of everything we think is negative and works against us. On the average, according to Helmstetter, people receive 148,000 negative messages before they reach the age of eighteen. It is not hard to imagine what happens when people carry such a negative attitude into adulthood.

If what Helmstetter said is true, it is no wonder that so much conflict abounds in the world, the church, Christian organizations and the Christian home. It may even be that conservative Christians receive more than the average number of negative messages. Why is that? We can get so caught up with being right and doing right that we have no time to be truly human; no time to let our inner being catch up with our pious oughts and shoulds.

Being Christian does not automatically make it any easier to talk positively about solving conflicts. Perhaps one reason people avoid talking about how to resolve conflict is that conflict is so painful. Because it is painful we fear it. We know what we ought to do or what another person wants us to do, but we find it hard to unleash the spirit to do it. That involves the fear of losing out to someone else and it also involves the potential guilt of failure. It may even require change!

Another reason some of us avoid thinking and talking about conflict solutions is that we do not understand it very well. We do not understand the conflicts going on inside us and therefore we do not know how to manage them. Most of the time we just try to avoid the pain they cause. We stuff those inner conflicts in the closet, hoping they will not appear again. But surprise of surprises, they reappear over and over and over again.

The purpose of this book, however, is not to spend time dealing with the painful side of conflict. Instead, the goal is to encourage you to find a way to overcome the negative impulses within you. It is also important to overcome those that exist between you and the persons with whom you interact. We want to help you think about conflict positively and creatively, so your personal life, your family life, your work life and your church life can be more wholesome, healthy and productive.

Definition of Conflict

We must begin by having a correct definition of "conflict." According to one dictionary, "conflict" is a Latin compound word that means "to strike together." The prefix *con* is Latin for "with" and the root word *fligere* means "to strike." When two or more objects, ideas or feelings strike against each other, or in some otherwise gentle (or not so gentle) way get too close to another person's sovereign territory, warning signals go out that conflict is occurring. Our obligation is to do something about it.

The ancient Chinese character for conflict is made up of two parts. One part denotes "challenge" and the other part indicates "opportunity." In the Bible, both Jesus and Paul speak of the conflict between darkness and light as an opportunity for redemptive activity. God is not willing that anyone should perish but that all should come to the light.

If we can put the three ideas of striking together, challenge providing us with opportunity and God's desire for redemption all into one short statement, we should be able to say that "when conflict occurs, differences collide in such a way that we have an opportunity to exercise the Christian gift of redemption."

That does not mean having or resolving conflict is ever easy or free of pain. Having different opinions than another person about something close to our hearts often pains us deeply. We need to hear what James Fairfield says in *When You Don't Agree*. "Conflict is natural, normal, neutral. . . . It can turn into disastrous ends, but it doesn't need to."[1] Conflict by itself is neither bad nor wrong nor sinful. The difference between the rightness and wrongness in any conflict is how we work out the conflict in our lives and relationships.

By studying the conflicts in the Bible we can see how clearly that works. In a recent study of the 133 biblical conflicts between persons, no less than fifty-five resulted in a negative consequence. Another fifty-nine resulted in a more positive experience. The other nineteen concluded in mixed results.[2] We will look at this material more closely in chapter five.

Before we move on to study the different types of conflicts, we need to remember that conflict is always very complex. For one thing, it deals with "my" wants and needs in contrast to "your" wants and needs. It has to do with my comfort in contrast to your comfort. It involves my view or perspective as it differs from yours. Finally, it involves the amount of flexibility and adaptability to change each of us has within.

One way to understand group conflict is to use the model

suggested by one manual prepared for pastors. Writing about congregational groups the authors state the following:

About five percent of the members will be Visionaries or Innovators, people who see new ways of doing things and who are immediately excited about the possibilities. Another fifteen percent will be the Strategists or Early Adapters. Once they hear the Visionaries talking about their dreams, they quickly begin to plan how to carry out these new ideas.

The majority of the congregation, about sixty percent, will be Status Quo people. They do not really want change, but will go along with strong leadership and the people who make the best impression on them.

Then there are the fifteen percent of the people who are Negative or Late Adapters. They do not want change and will resist it. If change takes place, they will often come along only when they see they have to. About five percent might be identified as Antagonists. They will fight change and seek to maintain their power and control.[3]

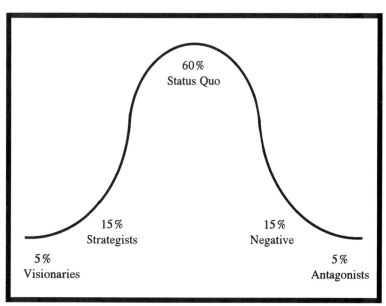

Change in Groups

The antagonists in one conflict are not necessarily the same people as the antagonists in other conflicts of that group. The personalities involved determine the antagonism to an idea or plan. It also depends upon how important the idea or plan is in relation to other issues in that person's life. We will explain this further in a later chapter.

Throughout this book new complexities of conflict will emerge. Just about the time you think you know everything there is to know about conflict, something new will leap out at you. Prepare yourself for an ever expanding horizon of knowledge. The more you know, the less you will be surprised by "things that go bump" in the heart.

Types of Conflict in Churches and Christian Groups

Many people think "a conflict is a conflict is a conflict." That is not so. Just as there are different varieties of oranges and many types of cacti in the desert or many varieties of evergreens in the forest, so also there are many kinds of conflicts.

For our purposes we will differentiate between three types or levels of intensity of conflict among people. The first is the ordinary, day-to-day, incidental type of disagreement that we all experience routinely and resolve quickly and simply. It could be compared to the giant cactus for which the Arizona desert is so popular. It can be seen everywhere and is not particularly harmful. In a church setting this can be illustrated by two Sunday school teachers quickly agreeing to rearrange the time schedule in a class period to fit the special needs of their students. In families and Christian groups of all sorts it has to do with negotiating many routine tasks of life.

A second type of conflict is one in which the disagreement can cause hurt feelings and bad talk. It reminds me of the prickly pear cactus, which can produce definite pain if a person falls into it. Imagine what would happen if the same Sunday school teacher mentioned above came breezing into class two minutes before starting time several Sundays in a row and each time tried to revise the class schedule to suit his/her own personal needs. The teaching partner would soon run out of emotional coping energy and would begin looking for ways to relieve the stress. Two ways of coping with that energy drain would be to answer negatively, or to talk to others about the pain and discomfort s/he was experiencing. That is how bad talk gets started.

Often those hurt feelings and unkind words create enough of a barrier between people so that resolution requires the help of a friend or associate. As shown above, such conflicts occur when one person presumes too quickly and too often upon another person's good graces. All of us have the ability to give and take a little, but there are limits to the stretching we want to do, or are able to do.

The third type of conflict occurs when the disagreement causes, or threatens to cause, a rupture in the relationship. It can be illustrated by the barrel cactus, which is smaller than the rest, but whose thorns very quickly puncture the skin. In the incident cited above, the one teacher may stop teaching to avoid the pain of repeated, surprise schedule changes, or may simply become apathetic and ineffective in his/her work.

This type of conflict occurs most often when one person or group inappropriately impinges opinions, ideas or decisions upon others. When enough personal offenses or attacks against a friend (or sometimes a valued object) occur, the offended party simply walks away from the conflict before it "does them in." Resolution for this type of conflict usually requires the help of a neutral, trained mediator.

Reasons for Conflict Among Christians

Besides understanding the different types of intensity of a conflict, reasons for conflict may be sorted out according to the impact they have upon our lives. One such impact is upon our **value system** which involves our most important ideas and beliefs about God, life, others and possessions. Within the same church or family group few conflicts occur over values, although a heterogeneous Christian organization may not be quite so fortunate. Let's look at some examples.

Biblical examples of value conflicts include the disagreement between Joseph and Potiphar's wife over the issue of marital integrity and the disagreement between the Pharisees and Jesus about his love for tax collectors and other social sinners.

Value issues today might include such things as sexual ethics, the sanctity of life, love for others and the solidarity of the church, group or family. They also may involve the way certain favorite persons or objects are treated.

Another reason for conflict relates to the way different **goals** introduce changes into our lives. Goals are the general targets at which we aim in order to experience positively the values we hold dear. When persons within a church or family group insist strongly on aiming at different goals, conflict can occur over goal selection.

In the Bible conflicts that relate to differences in goal orientation include David's attempt to take a military census. His goal was to attain a greater sense of personal and international security. Another goal-related conflict is illustrated by the disagreement between Jesus and the disciples over what kind of kingdom would best accomplish God's purposes here on earth.

Conflicts over goals often involve taking care of the established group at the expense of reaching out to new people (or vice versa). They also may include program ideas for which the whole group does not take ownership. Finally, they may involve issues of change that threaten established individual power and comfort. Conflicts over group goals probably occur more often than conflicts over group values.

A third reason for human conflict lies in the different **methods** by which we want to accomplish our group goals. This gets us down to the fine points of daily living. All groups can find some common values. In the course of everyday life, however, the goals they want and the methods by which they want to accomplish those goals become more conflictive as they descend in order of importance. Thus the differences in method cause us more problems than all other conflicts combined.

In the Bible, a conflict over methods once caused Moses to strike the rock to get water instead of speaking to it as God commanded. Another conflict caused Paul and Barnabas to part company while planning for the second missionary journey because they could not agree on how to use John Mark.

Conflicts in methods in our corporate organizational or church experience range from when to schedule an event to how fancy to make the renovation of the west wing to how much publicity to give to a special program. One committee member might want to limit the number of posters on the bulletin board and another might want to increase publicity over the radio. At home, one family member might squeeze the tube of tooth paste in the middle, while another might want everyone to roll it up neatly from the end.

Truly, if Jesus walked with us in the flesh, he would marvel at how inventive we are in finding ways to disagree with each other, making life more miserable in the process.

Major Conflict Management Styles

Conflict management experts generally identify five different conflict management styles, but this chapter will deal with only three. All five will be discussed in greater detail in chapter four.

Conflict management styles are the different ways by which people react to situations in life that are different from what they want or expect. Each of us has a preferred or "easier-than-any-other" conflict management style and a secondary or backup style. The backup style kicks in automatically if the first one is not effective.

The differences of style relate partly to the way in which we were individually created. Our genetic make-up predisposes us to react in certain ways. Our styles are also shaped by experiences and the pain we have encountered in life. In some very important ways this aspect of our personality is rooted more in the feelings than in the mind. This is especially true in relation to the way we handle our fears and expectations for future performance.

I do not mean to suggest that we are victims of circumstance, however. Many scriptures teach that God gives us the ability to control, guide and shape our habitual responses so they build up rather than tear down. The real task is to train our sensitivities to evaluate how we are managing our conflicts.

Of the five conflict management styles usually identified, the three approaches used most often in resolving conflicts are competition (I win, you lose), accommodation (I lose, you win) and collaboration (we both win something). The Scriptures illustrate all three of them, as we will see here and again in chapter four in more detail.

Competition is the position in which a person or group of persons declares in effect, "I/We want to have it my/our way this time. I/We must have it my/our way." They resolutely set about the task of overcoming the opposition by whatever method works best. Sometimes they go head to head. Other times they work quietly in the background. Still other times they size up the situation and deliver a volley of sidewinders that stab, humiliate and weaken people (and relationships) until very little of any value is left.

Such a style of conflict management leads either to ruptures or wars, or to demoralization, apathy and a passive stance in carrying out the mission of the church or organization. In the minds of the victors, they have brought the "enemy" under control. In reality, they have so neutralized and demoralized other persons that the full energy and power of God's Spirit cannot flow freely through any of them.

One biblical example of managing conflict by competition is the continual feud between Saul and David. The people elected Saul as king primarily to defend the Israelites against external enemies, such as the Philistines. His feud with David so weakened his government that it finally fell to the very enemy he was supposed to repel.

Another example is the sad division between Paul and Barnabas in Acts 15:36-40. Paul and Barnabas were a good team. The dynamic enthusiasm and clear insight of Paul, blended with the patient, quiet, tender loving care of Barnabas, made them irresistible in many strange cities. However, they could not agree about taking John Mark along on a second trip. That disagreement finally split the ace missionary team.

Accommodation, a second popular conflict management style, occurs when one person says to another, "Okay, I'll go along with you; you can have it your way this time." In reality that is a lose-win position. One person, created in the image of God, having godly ideas about how to solve a problem tucked quietly away within him/her, meekly goes along with the other to keep the peace.

Unfortunately, the price for that kind of peace may eventually include ulcers, severe headaches, chronic backache and many other physical illnesses. More seriously, in terms of solving problems in families, churches and Christian organizations, this approach also can lead to apathy and passivity and to the lack of creative involvement. Good, new ideas dry up very quickly when no one listens to them or appreciates them. Happily, however, when people use accommodation properly it can lead to genuine peace and at times it is the right response to a conflict.

The best biblical example of all shows how Abraham worked with Lot, trying to find a solution for settling the grazing rights for their respective cattle herds (Gen. 13). Abraham had control of that dilemma. He could have told Lot to move on. Instead, he chose to give Lot the choice of going or staying. To say it another way, he chose to let someone else choose. Yet, although he got the poorer grazing lands for his flocks, in the long run he lived a better and happier life than Lot did.

A much better method of conflict management is **collaboration**, or consensus building. Consensus is not necessarily the same as uniformity or unanimity in the whole group, although it could be. Consensus is establishing common, general, acceptable agreement within the group. It does not require a unanimous vote; it seeks common consent. It does not expect everyone to suspend their own personal judgments or feelings, but allows each to share their judgments and feelings in creating a better solution. Consensus says, "Let's talk about the *issues* and *values* that are at stake here, not only about our own personal interests. Let's keep on talking until we find the best solution possible for us all."

The process of seeking consensus makes it possible for *everyone* to express their own personal ideas and feelings about the issue. It allows people to become involved in building a sense of identity for the church/family/group in which they exist. It allows the whole group to construct an agreement with which everyone can live more comfortably than otherwise.

The best biblical example of collaboration is the apostles and other church leaders agreeing on a better way to care for the widows who were overlooked in the daily distribution of food in Acts 6. A close runner-up to that successful conflict resolution episode is the agreement between conservatives and progressives on the place of traditional Jewish values in the Gentile church. They forged that agreement at the Jerusalem Conference in Acts 15. It was not a perfect decision, as we will see later, but it nevertheless served the church well for a short time.

Collaboration is the servant leadership stance of superior conflict management that we will discuss in greater detail in chapter nine. It allows the leader to legitimate each person in the church, group or organization. It gives each an opportunity to interact with the other and thus to grow in Christ. That in turn allows them to take more ownership of the entire process of serving one another in love. Finally, it allows people in the group to give attention to the meanings and feelings of each other, as they learn the art of perception clarification.

Collaboration also requires that people work intentionally at building stronger relationships with each other. It is not satisfactory to rely on chemistry or natural relationships to bridge every gap that exists between people. Jesus calls us to be peace*makers*. Good relationships do not just happen. They must be constructed.

Finally, collaboration requires that we develop the fine art of empowerment. Not everyone in the group or church we belong to has the same power to assert themselves, but everyone should have the right to try. Some people are powerless because they are rendered powerless by others. They need to be delivered from that grip. Others are powerless for other reasons but need help in overcoming their lack of power. Collaboration makes it possible for the strong to help the weak instead of hindering them. It is the servant model of Christ.

----

1. James G.T. Fairfield, *When You Don't Agree: A Guide to Resolving Marriage and Family Conflicts*, Scottdale, Pa.: Herald Press, 1977, p.20.

2. Marlin E. Thomas, *A Study of Conflict in the Bible*, Colorado Springs, Colo.: Resources for Resolving Life's Issues, 1988. Also distributed by Kindred Press, Winnipeg, Manitoba, Canada.

3. Ron Dow et.al., *Training Course on Utilizing Conflict in the Church*, Topeka, Kansas: Congregational Development Committee, Christian Church in Kansas, 1991.

CHAPTER TWO

How Can Good People Do Bad Things to Each Other?

Conflict is Part of Real Life

Conflict is painful. It is painful in the church and out of the church. It is sometimes more painful and sometimes less painful, but it is always painful.

You cannot avoid conflict. You cannot avoid it in the world, you cannot avoid it in your family and you cannot avoid it in your church. You cannot avoid it in any Christian group. You cannot even avoid it within yourself. Like the weather, it is always present.

Also like the weather, conflict is not evil. Conflict can produce evil results, but it also can produce good results. In itself, conflict is not evil, but our reactions to conflict *can* be evil.

So what is conflict? As we already said in chapter one, conflict occurs whenever two or more persons have different points of view on any matter. Family members collide in the kitchen in the late afternoon trying to decide how five people are going to get to three places in two cars. Church members stand around after church wondering who will be the next casualty: the organist, the choir director, the Sunday school superintendent, the youth director, or the pastor. Employees of a Christian organization go quietly about their assigned tasks, stunned and in turmoil over the last three firings that came about after two staff members had another heated round of discussion.

Such scenes are not strange to anyone. Although we do not like it, they are a part of what we might call the "stuff of life." In the whirl and confusion of life, we often get caught by surprise and exclaim in amazement, "How could he do that?" Or, "I didn't think she was so unspiritual." Or, "That wasn't really me!"

All too frequently people exclaim in frustration, "We need a real revival."

Some conflict occurs as we encounter different desires and different points of view within other people. At other times, conflict occurs because people employ bad behavior to combat the pain they experience within themselves.

Sometimes conflict occurs because of the different ranges of intensity with which our energies flow within us. The differences in how Type A and Type B people carry out their work is one example. Another example is demonstrated by the "J" and "P" differences revealed in the Myers-Briggs Type Indicator.[1]

Finally, another source of conflict is found in the different ranges of adaptability each of us has in meeting the stresses of life and in handling the differences in other people. Whenever we are startled (caught by surprise), a healthy individual first investigates and then asserts him/herself in a positive manner. If the situation involves unhealthy individuals, the natural human reaction is annoyance, followed quickly by anger, then avoidance and finally submission.[2]

Sometimes people who have difficulty adapting are called "narrow." Although that may be true, the term is always relative and more pejorative than useful. It is better to recognize that early in life some people develop the capacity to be more adaptable, while others do not. It may even be possible to say that some people are born with a predisposition for adaptability whereas others are not. That possibility should create within us a wider range of tolerance for those persons who cannot adapt as readily.

It is helpful for me to reflect on the fact that some vocalists have a three-octave range, while some non-singers have a monotone range. However, such persons may have great ability to love beautiful things, do wonderful, creative work, or care deeply for people. Their monotone range does not diminish their value as persons or necessarily limit their commitment to the arts, though it may keep them out of the church choir.

In seeking to understand how conflict develops, the model given by Norman Shawchuck may prove to be extremely useful.[3]

The Conflict Cycle Tornado

When Pastor Bob took over the pastorate at First Church of the Open Bible, the congregation had great expectations. He seemed so relaxed and outgoing. They were sure he would not push new ideas onto them like their former pastor, Pastor Lyle, had done.

At the third meeting of the church board, when Pastor Bob questioned the lack of an outreach program, some board members immediately stiffened. They remembered their heated discussions with Pastor Lyle. Because Pastor Bob did not know about that issue, he did not even suspect a problem.

The older board members grunted something about new ideas not working very well in their community, while the newer board members enthusiastically endorsed the idea of a new program.

Within two or three months Pastor Bob noticed that the older members had become pitted against the younger members in what seemed to him to be a power play. Before long the younger members were recalling earlier times when older board members had resisted progress and the older board members were telling stories about how Pastor Lyle had tried to push all his "newfangled" seminary ideas onto them. Finally, after several months of uneasiness, the pastor preached a sermon entitled "Marks of Lethargy in the Church." He timed it to immediately precede the next monthly board meeting.

At that board meeting the two sides battled it out for over an hour. They finally agreed that the pastor and two or three (younger) board members would develop a new outreach program for the church, which the whole board would then review. The board grudgingly approved the new plan, but it never got off the ground.

1. Tension Development

The experience of Pastor Bob illustrates how a cycle of conflict develops. In his case, he unwittingly walked into a situation that the long-time board members had never satisfactorily resolved. When he brought up the idea of an outreach program, they became uncomfortable. Their internal, protective reaction against trouble was developing tension in their muscular structures. One board member noticed his hand beginning to tremble. Another began breathing more rapidly and a third slowly developed a headache.

These common, physical reactions to stress are not bad. In reality they are very good. They are the body's "early warning signs" created by God to help us detect real dangers to our well-being.

For example, if a bear lumbered out of the woods in the direction of a camper and his family, the camper would immediately spring into action. His muscles would flex into readiness, his breathing would accelerate, his heart rate would increase and additional adrenaline would be secreted into his system.

The same type of internal, physical preparations occur when one person says or does something that another interprets as a threat. The body cannot, by itself, distinguish between real dangers and events that only appear to be physical threats. Consequently it readies itself for an attack, just in case. The individual must discern between real dangers and perceived dangers.

That is where the "early warning system" comes into play. If we detect intensified physical functions occurring while a fire alarm is sounding, we do not tarry long to decide if we should escape from the building or not. We run.

Those same increased physical functions occur in a non-physically threatening situation. They can even occur in connection with something someone says in a group meeting. In such cases we usually have a few moments for reflection before "blowing up."

It is possible to train ourselves to react calmly under such circumstances, though inwardly we may be seething. The best technique I know of for buying time and gaining better control of ourselves is asking a question.

"What did you mean by _____?" or "Please explain your reasons for saying that," or "How do you think it might work here?" are examples of the questions that can help us buy time when internal physical tension begins to develop.

Nebuchadnezzar experienced terrible tension development when Daniel's three friends challenged his authority. In Daniel 3:19 we read, *Then Nebuchadnezzar was furious with Shadrach, Meshach and Abednego and his attitude toward them changed.* Unfortunately, the king did not manage his anger well and nearly destroyed three excellent servants of his court in the process.

2. Role Dilemma

If we do not find an acceptable way of buying time, we will inevitably move to the second stage of the conflict cycle, seeking to decide "who's in charge here?"

That second stage is illustrated by the standoff between the older and the younger members of the board at First Church. After many years of leading their church, the older board members truly felt they were doing things right. They had put a lot of voluntary time and effort into keeping their church open and were justifiably proud of their efforts. On the other hand, the more recently elected board members believed they had been elected to the board because of their own gifts of leadership and discernment. They believed they understood the contemporary needs of the church and the community and that their views and opinions counted for something.

When Pastor Bob came to the church, he believed his training and knowledge really had value. He knew what sacrifices he and his family had made to complete his seminary training. He also knew how hard his parents and his home church had prayed that God would supply their every need. He believed God had called him to First Church and wanted him to use his insights and gifts there to help the church reach out into its community.

The evening that Pastor Bob asked the church board about outreach, he noticed that some older board members fidgeted nervously. However, he did not understand exactly what that meant nor how deeply the question affected them. As a young pastor, he felt insecure in his efforts to deal effectively with older lay leadership. Above all else he certainly did not want to make any mistakes. The question about an outreach program was an honest question on his part and the board's lack of enthusiasm puzzled him.

The older board members, on the other hand, felt just as threatened as any camper would have been if a bear had begun to attack their campsite. They did not know what to do. They did not want to offend their new pastor. They truly believed, however, that their informal method of slowly assimilating new members into the church was not all that bad. They had lived through good times and bad times and felt they could say, without hesitation, which persons in the community were "reachable" and which ones were not. Their church had been there a long time and would remain a part of the community for a long time to come. They did not understand their new pastor's sense of urgency.

The newer board members were not battle-worn yet, nor fully integrated into the inner fabric of the traditions of the church. They eagerly wanted to make their mark in the world for Christ. They had been listening to their new pastor's excellent sermons calling for outreach and evangelism and wanted to put them into practice immediately.

Slowly the two sides began to polarize. The pastor began to feel his role as spiritual leader of the church was on the line. The older board members felt their many years of steady and mature guidance slipping away. The younger, more recent board members felt betrayed in their new roles as leaders.

For their own personal reasons, each person on the board silently began to ask the question, "Who's in charge in this church?" As threats to their personal integrity as board leaders seemed to become more apparent, their physical reactions to the unnamed fear became more pronounced and hard to control.

As this second stage of the conflict cycle neared its peak, it moved out of the range of effective pastoral management. There were no lay leaders left to participate in objective mediation and the "sides" became less desirous of fair arbitration.

Whenever people find themselves caught at such a stage of conflict, the safest recourse is to seek the help of an objective outside party. S/he should be one who can help bring balance and objectivity back into the relationship. A caring friend, a neutral "outside" pastor, denominational leaders, or a professional counselor can help in situations like this. They must know clearly what their real agenda and assignment is, however. Imposing an answer on the group is not enough. They must help the group develop its own answer to the problem.

If members of the group as a whole are not ready to seek such guidance, any concerned individual in the group may still seek out help for him/herself. A more neutral, balanced perspective is helpful for anyone in such a case. Such a person may then find ways to develop alternate problem-solving approaches which could become available to the whole group.

In the case of First Church, either an older board member, a newer board member, or the pastor could have approached a neutral observer and said, "We're having quite a disagreement in our board right now." The person could describe briefly what the disagreement was about and how the two sides were behaving. The person could then ask, "What are some ways I could respond differently, so we can make progress in our discussions and get the church back on track again?"

An excellent biblical example of how "role dilemma" destroyed relationships is in the standoff between King Ahasuerus and Queen Vashti in the book of Esther. The king wanted to revel in his own vanity regarding his queen, the queen wanted no part of the raucous crowd and the male advisors to the king felt their own male authority was hanging in the balance. For lack of good counsel this role dilemma ultimately proved to be fatal to all the parties involved in the dispute. Vashti lost her crown and the king ultimately got into trouble with the Jewish minority of the city. Esther's coronation led to Mordecai's promotion, which led to Haman's jealousy and attempt to eradicate all the Jews. Haman lost his head and the king lost a good servant.

3. Injustice Collecting

If the group, or an individual in the group, cannot arrest the conflict cycle at the second stage, it very quickly moves into the third stage. This is the stage of collecting individual injustices about persons on "the other side."

The older, more established side may begin complaining about the lack of experience of the younger leadership. They may see them as immature, spiritually inadequate, or out of touch with the deeper needs of the church. Sometimes they will use words such as "modernistic" or "humanistic" (or whatever the going fad word is at the time).

The newer members of the board may begin complaining about power blocs in the board. They may speak of cliques, narrowness and the lack of willingness to change. They may begin speaking of a need for revival and lament the willingness to "protect the church at all costs" instead of reaching out to new people. They may become lethargic and apathetic and eventually attend board meetings and church functions less frequently. They may even begin to talk about changing churches.

The new pastor will ultimately reach out in frustration to anyone who will listen to his pain and frustration. He may talk to some of the more sensitive, older members of the church, or he may share his struggle and frustration with newer members of the leadership team. In either case such sharing will serve only to polarize the two sides further. It will seldom solve any problems, bring any new perspectives, or improve communication between the people involved.

Still, without being able to share with someone, the pastor would soon begin to lose his own sense of identity and purpose in ministry. In a time like that he would find it absolutely necessary to verify his own ideas. He should seek the counsel of his district minister, although he would naturally be inclined to go to those who most nearly agreed with him and made him feel comfortable.

In a parachurch organization or a family group it is no different. Family members would tend to talk to other family members who sympathized with them and organizational sub-groups would tend to form around persons with like-minded ideas. In such cases each group changes their task from that of solving the problem to that of verifying "they are not wrong." As a result, both sides pile up arguments and accusations that fortify their own points of view.

At this stage in the conflict cycle there are only two ways to positively resolve the crisis and avoid the otherwise impending upheaval. The first is for enough members of the group to decide that keeping the group together is more important than splitting over that particular type of issue. They must be so strongly committed to keeping the whole body together that they are willing to do the hard work of active listening and truthtelling. Thus they can help the group forge the right kind of compromise as they surrender their own feelings of rightness for the sake of unity in the entire group.

The second way of resolving the crisis at this stage is to bring in an outside mediator who can do fair and equal listening for the whole group. Then s/he can help the group listen to each other the right way. If the members of the polarized group become willing to pay the price for such help (both in terms of surrendered pride and financial remuneration), it is possible with much care and guidance to unwind the conflict before it explodes.

An excellent biblical example of injustice collecting that ended in destruction for the injustice collector is King Saul's pursuit of David. At first Saul was grateful to David for vanquishing the giant, Goliath. In reward, the king added David to his bodyguard. However, as David's exploits brought him more and more fame, the king's jealousy grew until it mastered him. The king interpreted David's achievements and the accolades from the people as injustices against himself. Eventually

David was forced to become an outlaw of the court, unable to serve King Saul any longer.

4. Confrontation

Conflicts which are not resolved in a fair and just manner finally lead to "war." When enough injustices have been collected by one side or the other, missiles begin to fly. They may be dispatched through the informal communications network (gossip), through innuendoes in bulletin announcements or newsletter clips, through barbs in conversations and public meetings, or through burdened prayer requests in solemn church assemblies.

When Pastor Bob finally reached his frustration saturation level with the board, he felt compelled to take some kind of action. He reasoned that he was the spiritual leader of the church. As such he needed to call the church out of its lethargy and sin to a full and active obedience to Christ.

The Sunday he preached his sermon on "Marks of Lethargy in the Church" the younger half of the church applauded him as they left the sanctuary. However, the older leaders shuffled by silently and then gathered in small clusters in the foyer and the parking lot. They could not understand why their pastor would attack them from the pulpit after all the years of hard work they had done for the Lord.

That week, when the board met, the air was tense. The pastor's devotional thoughts centered on being open to the Lord. The older members definitely thought he meant they should be open to his version of the Lord's will.

After the board finished its preliminary business, discussion centered on developing an evangelistic outreach program. The younger members were all fired up by this time and aggressively promoted their pastor's ideas. One older member remarked, "If that's what you mean by being sensitive to the Lord, count me out. I've been serving the Lord for over twenty years and I've never been called insensitive before. Besides, Pastor, you're just going too fast for me."

For the next hour board members lobbed accounts of previous injustices at each other. Finally, a more moderate board member moved that those members who favored the new proposals form a committee with the pastor to develop a comprehensive plan of action. The motion carried reluctantly.

At the next regular meeting the board passively approved the new plan and the pastor and his supporters began implementation of it. However, by then everyone in the church was so tired of the tension that had developed they did not have any enthusiasm left to put the plan into action.

One alternate way for resolving the problem in a more positive manner would have been for someone to introduce the idea of a three-month trial period for a new outreach program. Such a compromise could have come early in the conflict, before the pastor reached his saturation level. He may not even have thought about a sermon on lethargy in the church if that had happened. Either he or one of his supporters could have brought such a compromise to a board meeting, rather than holding out for full compliance by everyone at the same time.

It happens very rarely that everyone in a group is ready for change at the same time. The wise leader is the one who will seek a compromise, an interim solution while people have a chance to rethink their positions. That way everyone can evaluate the early outcomes of the program.

Many years ago Lawrence Richards pointed out that every group contains a minority which opposes all change, an opposite minority which is always ready for change and a vast majority which will approach change very cautiously. This majority wants to be sure it will work before they try it.[4] This is similar to the bell-shaped curve introduced in the previous chapter (page 7).

A clear biblical example of confrontation is Absalom's attempt to take the throne from his father David. The biblical evidence is clear that David did not use the abilities of his sons very well, nor did he discipline them wisely. When Absalom's pile of injustices concerning the rulership of Israel reached its peak, he gathered his supporters and in return David gathered his loyal troops about him. In the conflict that followed, Absalom lost his life. David returned to the throne so weakened that he was unable to accomplish any additional great achievements.

5. Adjustments

No matter how the confrontation occurs, adjustments will automatically take place. This will be true in the relationships of the people involved and in the way the organization functions. There will be choices to make in those adjustments. Either people will choose to make an adjustment that improves communication, relationship and function, or they will fail to choose. Failure to choose (choosing by default) will inevitably result in following the flow of one's feelings. That in itself can result in either a good or a bad outcome.

A negatively oriented series of conflict cycles with no positive learnings or changes in behavior.

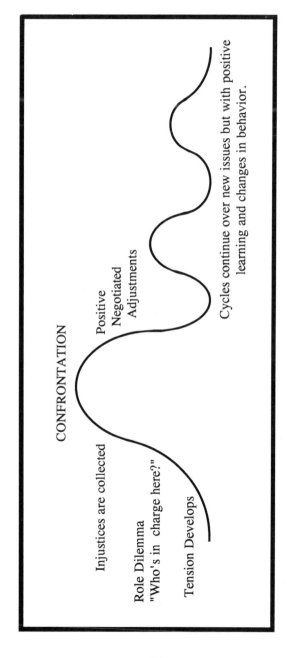

Injustices are collected

Role Dilemma
"Who's in charge here?"

Tension Develops

CONFRONTATION

Positive
Negotiated
Adjustments

Cycles continue over new issues but with positive
learning and changes in behavior.

A positively oriented series of conflict cycles.

Among the choices from which to select are submission, passive compliance, active compliance and leaving. In submission, the person or persons who lose the struggle may either submit willingly or unwillingly. If they submit willingly their actions will strengthen the work of the Lord through their church. If they submit unwillingly, they will unwittingly begin piling up injustices all over again in preparation for the next round of conflict.

In compliance, the persons know they do not agree with the decision. They also know, however, that their cooperation with the church or Christian group they are a part of is important for its healthy survival and progress. This is better than submission, for the individuals come to terms with their feelings about the decision and voluntarily choose to cooperate. It makes their cooperation more genuine and longer lasting.

There is a difference between passive compliance and active compliance. In passive compliance the person agrees to let the program go forward under the leadership of others, but does not get personally involved. In active compliance the person agrees to stay involved in the program, although it was not his/her own program of choice.

Sometimes it is difficult for people to participate fully in an event or activity they do not support. If they then choose to support it passively that is not totally negative, especially if they do it out of knowledge and in an agreeable spirit. Churches need to come to the point where they can give permission to others to do things without having 100 percent agreement first.

The other option is the choice of leaving. Leaving is always painful, but it is sometimes the most honest choice. A person must be able to live with his/her conscience. Paul recognized that in Romans 14:14, 23.

However, although leaving is sometimes the most honest choice, it also may be the least mature choice. The only way that can be decided is to determine what is "the higher good" in the individual's mind. If the higher good is defending one's honor or standing firm on one's view, there is no other choice but to leave. However, if the higher good is the development of the body of Christ, then it is better to stay and work together so the body of Christ does not become more fragmented.

We should not think that after a group has successfully resolved one major conflict it will never have another one. We speak of the conflict cycle because it is just that. Conflict is always cyclical in nature. If one conflict gets resolved poorly, its unfinished issues and feelings will come up again later, either in the same form or in another one. Even if the conflict gets resolved well, another conflict will eventually take its place. That is the way life is.

However, if the group chooses to learn something about conflict resolution while working through one conflict, succeeding conflicts will not seem so severe or be as difficult to resolve. Just as in any other issue of life, one lesson well learned improves the quality of life. On the other hand, a lesson ignored sets the stage for the next round of difficulty.

Take, for example, the lesson Paul learned when he and Barnabas parted company in Acts 15:39. Although it was a painful lesson to learn, he adjusted well and did not lose his future ministry because of it. Moreover, he was better able to use his team members on subsequent missions and even recognized the value of John Mark many years later. It became a much more profitable lesson for him than King Saul's experience or King David's conflict with Absalom.

---

1. See chapter seven.

2. Stanley Keleman, *Emotional Anatomy*, Berkeley: Center Press, 1985.

3. Norman Shawchuk, *How to Manage Conflict in the Church*, Irvine, Calif.: Spiritual Growth Resources, 1983, vol. I:35-37.

4. Lawrence O. Richards, *A New Face for the Church*, Grand Rapids: Zondervan, 1970, pp. 42-43.

CHAPTER THREE

The Five Deepening Levels of Conflict

In chapter two we described the five stages of a conflict cycle and suggested that one conflict cycle usually follows another.

In this chapter we will see how that works. We will come to understand that if a group does not resolve an organizational conflict satisfactorily, it will eventually cycle into another similar conflict, probably of greater intensity. The players may be similar or different and the issue may or may not be the same. The negative energy and the underlying causes, however, will likely be similar if not identical to the previous cycle.

As the cycles continue over time, they will tend to get both tighter and uglier. People will have less patience with each other's differences and the cycles will not take as long to complete. Moreover, the social graces that may have marked the earliest conflicts will no longer be present.

The tightening cyclical nature of organizational conflict may occur within the lay leadership of a church or within any department of it. It also may occur between succeeding pastors and the lay leadership of the church or between any persons or group of persons in a parachurch organization.

If it occurs between a succession of pastors and the lay leadership of the church, those pastors who enter a conflicted congregation will unknowingly fall heir to a system of injustice collecting and confrontation with which they are unfamiliar. They will likely not survive for long in such a climate. The same may be true for succeeding leaders in parachurch organizations.

As we study more fully the five deepening levels of group conflict, we will notice how subtly and insidiously simple issues may turn into painful group conflicts and even massive crusades, which can imperil witness and destroy lives. In this discussion we are deeply indebted to the original work of Speed Leas, who first identified the five levels of conflict in a church.[1]

It would be helpful, as you study this chapter, to keep in mind the deepening conflict which Samuel and Saul experienced in 1 Samuel 13, 15 and 28. Samuel was the prophet who selected Saul and anointed him as the first king of Israel. In two successive stages Saul sought to appropriate power that did not belong to him. He consistently refused to acknowledge and correct his mistakes. As a result he lost contact with Samuel and eventually lost his right to found a dynasty.

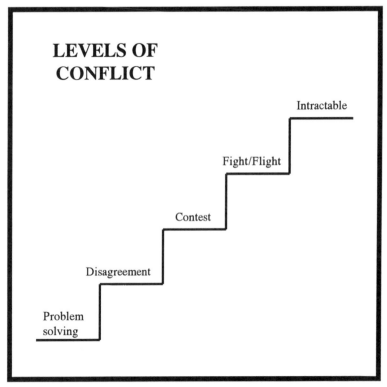

LEVELS OF CONFLICT

Intractable

Fight/Flight

Contest

Disagreement

Problem solving

Conflict Level One:
Problems to Solve

As we have already said earlier, conflict is part of "the stuff of life." It is always with us. The pastor faces it when he has to decide whether to cancel Sunday services because of a blizzard, flood, or earthquake and the Sunday school superintendent encounters it when s/he rearranges the classroom locations to accommodate an overflow crowd in one class.

As long as we view our conflicts as problems which need to be solved and not as contests of the will or validations of ego, conflicts are our friends. They help us move through life in an orderly, creative and constructive manner. They help us make life better for everyone. Otherwise, they may destroy us.

Finances were a real problem at Elm Street Church. Oliver made the assumption that turning out lights was the right way to conserve money and began actively promoting the idea. Others either agreed with him or did not want to upset him. They reasoned that the dollars saved would provide additional resources for precious Christian education materials.

As time went by Elm Street Church made several strategic mistakes. No one ever bothered to find out how significant the savings on the electrical bill really were as other operational costs skyrocketed. The sense of satisfaction which people derived from turning out lights evolved into a sense of mission.

Another crucial mistake was that the practice of conserving energy carried over into keeping track of how many lights were left on in the parsonage and how often the office copier was left running. That inevitably encroached upon the private lives and responsibilities of other persons, including the pastor's family and the office secretary. Without being aware of what was happening, an earlier positive approach to conflict resolution turned into a deadly decline in a sense of what was the real mission of the church.

There are several rules for managing conflict at the Level One stage. These can help keep conflict in its proper perspective and allow it to contribute to the life and development of the church.

1. **Report** your ideas and feelings about group life to others before acting unilaterally on any of them. Do not assume others think or feel the same way you do until they clearly say so.

2. Take time to let others **repeat** back to you their feelings and thoughts about your proposals. Make sure they understood what you intended and that you understand any variations in their perspective.

3. **Review** all the options available to the group, so the problem can be fixed as well as possible with the most acceptable results for everyone.

4. **Reevaluate** the results periodically to make sure the solution to the problem is still working well. Make adjustments as needed.

In the light of these four rules, it is easy to see how Elm Street Church gradually moved from being a struggling but effective church to one that experienced a state of apathy and stagnation. Had Oliver and others carefully followed the four rules listed above, the conflict that eventually ruined more than one pastor's ministry would not have occurred.

The early church handled the conflict between the Greek and Jewish widows in Acts 6 in this mature style. The people brought their complaints to the apostles, who listened to the concerns and invited the lay leadership to seek solutions. They did all of it in a spirit of collaboration and the problem apparently was resolved easily.

Conflict Level Two:
Disagreements Which Lead to Discomfort

A good solution to a Level One problem is one in which everyone owns part of the solution. They do not have to own equal parts of the solution, but they have to feel the real problem was solved in a way that satisfies everyone. They need to be able to say in subsequent conversations, "We did a good job of solving that problem." Then it can be put to rest.

If people in conflict cannot reach such an agreement, those left out will eventually experience a Level Two conflict within themselves. It will be one in which they feel so uncomfortable that acquiescing to the will of the majority ceases to be an option for them.

That is what happened eventually to the secretaries and the steady stream of pastors passing through the Elm Street Church. It is also what had happened to Pastor Lyle and the board of First Church in chapter two of this book. At Elm Street Church there was an avoidance of the problem and at First Church there was no agreement on the nature of the problem that some of them felt the church faced.

At Level Two the emphasis shifts from problem solving to ego-protection. Individuals have more interest in proving their point than in helping the church move forward. Self-validation becomes more important than the total mission of the church. People who feel unjustly set aside begin to gather troops around themselves. They do this partly to bolster their views, partly to prove their point more forcefully and partly to aid in advancing their strategies.

Another symptom of a Level Two conflict is a shift from specific language about the conflict to generalizations of the issue. No longer do they name individuals with whom they disagree or state specifically what the disagreements are. They speak instead of "some people around here" or "several vocal critics," and refer to "issues of serious concern to many people." They begin to speak of a lack of trust, a problem in communication, a lack of commitment, or unspiritual attitudes in the church.

It is possible to intervene locally in a Level Two conflict before it grows into an even greater problem. There are several important rules to follow if it is to be successful.

1. Any individual in the group may initiate an intervention, but s/he must be committed, objective and intentional in his/her efforts. In addition, s/he must know when to go for outside help.

2. The individual who wants to intervene must be one who has the ear of the wounded parties in the church. S/he also must be able to gain the attention of "the other side." Matthew 18:15-17 only works when both parties feel they will be heard equally.

3. The intervener must take a neutral stand in the quest for resolution. It must be more important to bring understanding and unity to the group than to resolve the issue one way or another.

4. The intervener must be sensitive to the feelings and concerns of all parties involved in the conflict, without betraying the trust of any.

5. The intervener must secure accurate, reliable, objective information. It is not necessary to uncover every detail, but it is important to generate essential information that may aid in decision-making. The reporter's questions–Who, What, When, Where and How–are helpful here. (Only after these five questions are satisfied may the Why question be raised. If it is presented too early in the process, moralizing and second-guessing can too easily replace accurate information gathering.)

6. The intervener must then encourage parties on both sides of the conflict to recognize the issue objectively for what it is. S/he must be able to lead them to a solution that is at least one step higher than the level of the problem they were addressing.

For example, if the issue is a goals-oriented issue, it is likely that the conflict had begun to focus on methodologies or personalities. In such an instance it should be solved at the values level. Robert Terry of the University of Minnesota has wisely observed that "whatever the problem is, it is really the next level up . . . and we tend to solve it the next level down."[2]

7. The intervener must be ready to get help when the first efforts at intervention do not succeed. Waiting too long to get additional help may aggravate the problem. Here the maxim must be, "If at first you don't succeed, seek the collaboration of another helper."

Abraham's successful attempt at resolving a dispute between his herdsmen and Lot's herdsmen in Genesis 13 is an example of an individual within the dispute being able to resolve a difficult situation. Although the two groups of herdsmen were not able to continue using the same pastures, the two families were able to remain friends.

Conflict Level Three:
Contest Between Potential Winners and Losers

An adequate, satisfactory resolution to a Level Two conflict must allow the persons who felt left out of previous decision-making efforts to feel a part of the group again. It must allow time for feelings to heal sufficiently so that complete trust can be restored. The old party lines must be diffused and people must again talk freely and intimately about their minor grievances as well as their joys.

If such resolution and mending does not occur, it will only be a matter of time before conflict at Level Three breaks out into the open.

A Level Three conflict is one in which individuals feel they have given in long enough and often enough and now deserve to win one. They are not ready yet to wound individuals or tear the fabric of the church apart, but they do not merely want to be the gracious losers time after time. It may also occur when individuals feel their values and traditions are seriously at risk and they do not want to compromise them for the convenience of others.

Consequently, a Level Three conflict follows several rounds of Level One and Level Two conflict. It is fortified by a volume of injustices that have been collected and stored up over a period of many years.

A Level Three conflict may break out so suddenly that it surprises a new pastor, departmental leader, or board member who did not know enough of the history of the group to suspect anything as awesome as this could be brewing. It could even surprise some old-timers, who had always "thought better of" the persons involved in the new conflict.

A clear indicator of a Level Three conflict is distortion in the way people talk about the current stress they are encountering.

Those persons who become the major players in the conflict present the immediate problem as much greater and more severe than others believe it to be. Then they pile up further injustices when "the other side" downplays the significance of what they say is so. Clearly they are so sore inside they can no longer contain themselves. It has to come out somehow, sometime.

Several types of distortions begin to appear at this level of a conflict and continue to escalate as the conflict moves into Levels Four and Five. One of them is *magnification*. Magnification occurs when an individual sees him/herself as the savior of the church or group. S/he begins to view the persons on the other side as the perpetrators of error or evil. It is a clear case of magnifying the sliver in another's eye and ignoring the beam in one's own eye.

Another type of distortion is *dichotomization*. That is the tendency to divide everything and everybody into stark black and white images. There is the group in favor of the issue and there are "many people" opposed to it. There is the spiritual group and the unspiritual group. There are those who are on the verge of leaving and those who will stay and fight to the finish. (Actually, it is too soon to begin to divide people up like this, although some may try. Such division does not actually occur until well into the fourth level.)

Over-generalization is another type of distortion characteristic of a Level Three conflict. It manifests itself in terms like Everyone, Nobody, You always and S/he never. It focuses on those times when opponents show their bad intentions and ignores those times when they show their loyalty to the church or group.

A fourth distortion is *assumption,* when people take the liberty of implying motives for things that others do and say without exploring the situation deeply enough to know all the facts. They make assumptions based on limited knowledge and lots of feelings and get offended when someone attempts to correct them.

The only way a pastor or any other individual from the group can arrest a Level Three conflict before it inflicts permanent damage is to assume the posture of a Moses and deliver God's people from bondage with a mighty hand. The danger is, however, that in so doing they may "slay an Egyptian" first. At this stage Matthew 18:17 will hardly bring the group together again, for fair and impartial judges are not easy to find in a hurting group or congregation.

A better option is for someone in the group to rise up as an unnamed prophet and, following the manner of the church leaders in Antioch (Acts 15:2), call for outside help. This also may be seen as an appeal to Matthew 18:17 with objective, outside arbitrators in charge. The outcome will be much more positive and wholesome.

Several steps are necessary for satisfactorily resolving a Level Three conflict. Among them are the following:

1. Active listening is a priority of the first order. Every hurting individual must be heard, whether in a group session or individually. They must be heard at the factual level but also at the emotional level. They must come to believe that both their feelings and ideas count and that they will not be run over in the process of mediation and reconstruction.

2. Clarification of all the pertinent facts must come into the domain of the intervener. This includes a history of the conflicts that have been a part of the church or group life for the past number of years and a profile of the types of leadership the church has experienced. It also may include information about the demographics of the church community, the document of call of the resident pastor or leader and the current goals statement of the group or congregation.

3. In a context of developing mutual trust, all persons who are party to the conflict must be willing to submit to the pertinent facts as gathered by the intervener. They must then be willing to return to the stated mission and goals statement of the church and commit themselves to pursuing that goal together.

4. Healing must be provided for wounded individuals and training in churchmanship and group process also must be available for the whole group or church. This can be done either through specialists brought in for that purpose or through a trained, intentional interim pastor (if the resident pastor chooses not to stay).

5. Finally, training in communication and decision-making skills, mutual support and fellowship groups and empowerment of all the laity must follow. In this way the spirit of conflict that lived in the group may die and not return to cause more damage.

The way in which the church at Antioch resolved its difficult conflict over circumcision in Acts 15 is a good example of one church seeking outside help. When there was a "sharp dispute" between the traveling conservative teachers and Paul and Silas (vv. 1-2), the church sent them to Jerusalem to seek mediation. There the entire church listened to all the views and also to stories of evangelism and church growth. Eventually James, the leading elder, summarized the conclusions. This course of action brought essential peace and unity to the church.

Conflict Level Four:
Fight to the Finish or Flee in Disgust

If a Level Three conflict is not resolved satisfactorily, it can either die down again or move immediately into a Level Four conflict. If some key person in the conflict gives in or leaves, it probably will die down for awhile. However, if no one budges it can quickly develop into a full-scale Level Four contest. People on both sides of an issue are so thoroughly convinced they are right and the other side is wrong that they give up trying to reason with each other or even trying to win them over. The only object left is to win the war.

The reasons for winning may be as diverse as the people who are part of the conflict. Some may want things to remain unchanged. Others may want major change. All believe their way of seeing things is the way God sees it.

Some hold out for a certain type of doctrinal purity. Others want to have their chance in the sun for leadership. The opposition fears giving them any real power. At the root of it all is the inability to negotiate differences successfully. At this level it is too late to negotiate; that should have been done at Level One or Two.

The intensity with which people pursue their goals also increases. They have endured so many injustices and the other side has committed so many offenses that it is now time' to punish. Obviously each person or group sees themselves as the instruments of God in carrying out that punishment.

Punishment can take several forms. It may be done by removing someone from office. Or it may be done by holding someone up for public ridicule or censure. It may even occur by totally ejecting someone from the group in a self-righteous act of purging out the old leaven.

It is usually at this stage that people draw the lines tightly both for the pastor and against the pastor, or any other vulnerable leader in the organization. There may have been insinuations already at Level Three that the pastor or leader is ineffective and should leave. At this level those insinuations become outright demands.

If the pastor or leader leaves under these circumstances, long term and sometimes even permanent damage is done to a pastoral or leadership family committed to the service of God. Moreover, the church or group merely sets itself up for another round of even more difficult conflict later in the future.

It is much better to have an outside analyst come in. For one thing, s/he can help the group understand itself better. Then, after things have settled down, s/he can help the group develop a more objective way to decide when and under what circumstances a leader should leave.

The language in a Level Four conflict changes from generalization at Level Two and distortion at Level Three to categories of ideological absolutes. Members of the various subgroups no longer talk about differences of opinion or even the gross injustices of the other side, but of absolute truth and error.

They suddenly know more about the important topics that govern faith, life and polity in the church than any other church leader they ever knew. They cite scripture passages to bolster their views without being open to other scriptures that cast a different light on the subject. They tout books, articles and papers that support their views. They declare that "if Rev. or Dr. or Mr. Senior Elder sees it this way, it's good enough for me." They see members of the opposition as unspiritual, liberal (or too conservative), uneducated, selfish, insensitive, not open to reason, or too spiritually immature to count.

It is probably impossible to salvage the entire ship when it is caught in the throes of a Level Four conflict. The pastor or leader is too wounded and the parties on all sides have too much at stake for everyone to begin over with a clean slate. However, if someone must leave, that leave-taking should occur as gently and carefully as possible, although it will not occur without pain.

The most strategic thing a pastor or leader can do with a Level Four conflict is to collect as much objective data as possible on all sides. He should call in two or three local support people to evaluate and either corroborate or revise what they sense to be true. They might then consult with denominational leaders to discern how best to help the church move beyond its stalemate.

Several options are open at this point. With denominational or organizational support, the pastor or leader can seek as good a transition to another assignment as possible. Alternately, he can bring top level executives in to assess the situation again and to confer briefly with the leaders of all factions in the church or group.

A third option is to suspend normal pastoring, gear up for specialized ministry and attempt to treat the sick system personally.[3] A fourth option is to discover a way to bring in an outside consultant or intervener. The hope here is that the sickness of the system can be addressed more thoroughly and healed more completely.

How does one call in outside help at this stage of the conflict?

1. Anyone can initiate such a call. However, that person should always act in tandem with other persons in the church and not by him/herself.

2. First, that individual (pastor, leader, troubled board member, or other concerned person) should go to the governing board of the church or group. The presentation should be somewhat as follows:

"I do not like the tension that exists in our church or group. I do not like to see people taking sides against each other. I do not like the way our mission to win the lost is being sacrificed in the interests of winning other types of battles. It seems we are at a stalemate and I would like very much to encourage the board to get some outside help. If you wish, I will help you do that, but please do something and do it soon."

3. If the governing board refuses to act, the concerned individual should confer with two or three others in the church or group and then contact denominational or organizational leaders. Their presentation should be similar to the one described above. If action is forthcoming in either case, they

should then graciously bow out and let the elected leadership give guidance to the intervention. They may participate only as concerned individuals and interviewees.

4. If denominational leaders cannot develop a course of action, there is one more possible step to take. The concerned individual may contact an intervener, describe the problem as s/he sees it and ask for advice. If the intervener is able to develop a course of action, there is still some hope. If not, it soon becomes obvious that the conflict is moving toward a Level Five conflict.

Isaac's attempt to quiet the recurring unrest between his family and Abimelech (see Gen. 21 and 26) is one example of how it is possible to assume a strong leadership role in resolving differences. In Isaac's case, of course, the decision was to move on (avoidance). The experience of Titus on Crete (Titus 1:5, 10-13) may be an early example of sending in an intervener to settle what could not be resolved peacefully by the local leadership.

Conflict Level Five:
Intractable Situations

Speed Leas has labeled the fifth level of conflict as intractable because the participants in the conflict are no longer able, even remotely, to manage it themselves. The conflict is managing them.

A Level Five conflict occurs when all (or at least most) parties in the conflict become so strong and so convinced they are right that no one is willing to give in or leave. They take on the aura of a crusader striving with all their might for what is right, plunging blindly forward no matter the destruction it brings in its wake.

It is at this point that Kenneth Haugk's insightful work, *Antagonists in the Church*, can prove to be helpful. Haugk describes the spiritual burden of those persons who first seek solace and comfort in the church and then eventually turn on the church and cause it undue pain.[4]

When a pastor gets caught in the throes of a Level Five conflict, there is no alternative for him but to expose it for what it really is, providing he himself is not a part of it.

1. He should first remove himself emotionally from the issues of the conflict and recognize he is dealing with forces beyond the normal scope of daily pastoral ministry.

2. He should quickly develop a strong professional support group for himself. He should gain as much insight and knowledge as he can about the psychological and spiritual dynamics of the conflict.

3. Then he should share his insights carefully with trusted and respected leaders in his congregation and with denominational officials. He also should have recourse to psychological consultants who can advise and guide him in the pursuit of his added responsibilities.

4. Next, he should take whatever appropriate measures are available to him.

   A. He may choose to resign, but should do so in such a way that the conflict does not continue unabated after he leaves.

   B. He may choose to approach the problem as one that is in need of demonic exorcism. If so, he should only do so with guidance and support from others. Even at that, it should only be with the greatest spiritual care and with the consent of the individuals involved.[5]

   C. A better approach in the mind of this author is to develop caring ways to remove temporarily a troubled individual from office in the church where s/he can do extreme damage. Then it is important to develop a caring ministry of active listening until his/her pain lessens and s/he can be channeled into appropriate long-term spiritual care. When ready, s/he should be returned to active service again.

Occasionally a pastor or leader causes major problems for a church or organization. If that is so, those around him who care for him may themselves follow the steps outlined above. The spiritual life of the church must be cared for, but the spiritual and emotional well-being of the pastor (or leader) and his family also must be an issue of concern. Only in very intractable cases should denominational leaders be called in to help local lay leaders in taking more drastic measures.

The story of Ananias and Sapphira in Acts 5 is one example of how an apostolic leader dealt with an intractable situation. The excommunication by Paul of a blatantly sinning believer, reported in 1 Corinthians 5 and 2 Corinthians 2, is another. It is clear in this second example that people had worked with the man and possibly even Paul himself had written to him earlier. It is also clear that when the man repented, the church restored him to full fellowship. Such restoration is still something many of us find hard to do. It would be good for us to develop enough courage to do it graciously in the spirit of Christ.

---

1. Speed Leas, *Moving Your Church Through Conflict*, Washington, D.C.: Alban Institute, 1985, pp.19-22.

2. Dr. Robert Terry, Director of the Reflective Leadership Program, Hubert H. Humphrey Institute of Public Affairs, University of Minnesota, Minneapolis, in a lecture reported to this author by a seminar participant.

3. See Marlin E. Thomas, "The Pastor's Role in Managing Church Conflict," *Direction*, 19:2 (Fall 1990) pp. 65-74.

4. Kenneth C. Haugk, *Antagonists in the Church: How to Identify and Deal with Destructive Conflict*, Minneapolis: Augsburg, 1988, pp.57-87.

5. See M. Scott Peck, *People of the Lie*, New York: Simon and Schuster, 1983, pp.182-212.

CHAPTER FOUR

Five Conflict Management Styles

Mention conflict and the first thing that comes to most peoples' minds is fear. Other words may include fight, anger, rage, disagreement, destruction and pain.

Intuitively, conflict is something we would like to avoid, yet we know that in this life it is not possible. What we find hard to fathom is how to face conflict so we are not always hurt by it.

In the previous two chapters we learned how conflict begins. We also saw how it escalates through five different stages and how it intensifies over time by moving through several different levels. In this chapter we want to learn something about the different ways people react to conflict. Again, there are five different styles of conflict management to consider.

We know, just by looking around us, that some people react more violently than others to conflict, while other people never seem to be troubled by it. They can take nearly everything in stride. We envy them, wishing we could do the same. At the same time, we struggle with those who cannot hold their anger, wishing there were a magic way to tame their spirits.

How does conflict management work? What can each of us do to remain more calm and controlled in the face of the "surprises" of life? When problem upon problem piles upon us, how can we maintain our balance without "losing it" and hurting those we love? How can we get through a church business meeting or a tense committee or board session without having very unchristian thoughts about those who create severe unrest and discord?

Conflict management has been a theme of contemporary literature now for nearly thirty years, but it has not crept into the conservative Christian vocabulary until very recently. Lloyd Perry, James Fairfield and Joseph Strayhorn, Jr. all wrote of it in 1977. Norman Shawchuck and Speed Leas first applied its terminology to church conflict in 1983-84.[1]

No single method for managing conflict is always superior to any other, for there are times when each of the five conflict management styles must be employed. Yet such evaluation tools as the Thomas-Kilmann Conflict Mode Instrument can help us discover what our preferred style is.[2] It also can help us discover how we will likely react to conflict in most situations.

The biblical and theological support for the five conflict management styles will be presented in the next chapter. Here, however, we want to describe how each style works and how it affects relationships. We will begin with what I regard as the most basic and original of the five styles (see diagrams on pages 45 and 46) and work our way toward the most developed and refined of them all.

Avoidance

The most basic, instinctual drive of the human being is the drive for survival. It is illustrated in many ways in the Scriptures. These include Cain and Abel's battle for supremacy and Esau's request for lentils from Jacob's kitchen. It also includes the Lord's Prayer with its request to supply us daily with enough bread to eat.

There is really no desire within humanity for conflict if that particular conflict may deprive a person of survival or of a peaceful existence. The only exceptions are if survival or peace is jeopardized by external forces, or if threats overwhelm the person.

Consequently, like the meek turtle,[3] a person will avoid a confrontation or conflict if it is in his/her best interests to do so. Adam and Eve at first avoided the confrontation with God, Abraham avoided confronting the Pharaoh when he wanted to have Sarah and David avoided confrontation with Saul in the Old Testament.

In the New Testament Joseph fled to Egypt to avoid encountering Herod's soldiers. Jesus avoided his brothers' challenge to "go up to Jerusalem that all men may see you" until several days after they had left. Finally, Paul and Silas at first avoided the loud cries of the Philippian girl who dogged their footsteps in Acts 16.

Avoidance is one natural coping skill built into the soul of every human being, even though it has the devastating effect of causing the other to feel rejected. It is literally impossible to interact meaningfully with every stimulus that comes our way everyday. We must be able to block some things out to survive.

Avoid

Accommodate

Compete

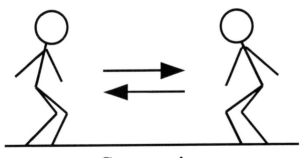

Compromise

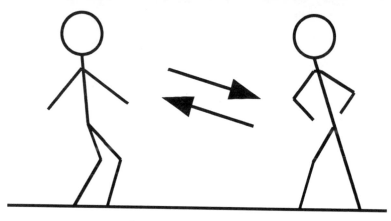

Accommodate

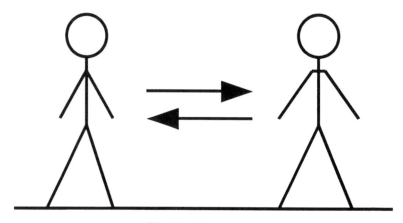

Collaborate

Avoidance, used at the right time and in the right way, is one means of improving our chances for survival and sanity. It requires little or no attention on our part. It allows the human body to go about its task of being, without spending anymore than a minimum amount of energy coping with stressful situations. In terms of conflict management, avoidance says to the intruder or challenger, "I'm leaving now; it's all up to you. The problem is all yours."

Avoidance was the technique used by the pastors of Elm Street Church to deal with the church's preoccupation of counting light bulbs. To them it just did not seem to be worth fussing about.

Accommodation

If avoidance does not effectively deal with all the stress points in our life, it is possible to accommodate some of them. Like the lovable teddy bear, we are able to absorb some negative aspects of other people and love them in spite of themselves.

Abraham accommodated Lot when their servants quarrelled over the vast pasture lands of the Judean slopes. Jesus accommodated his mother Mary when she reported there was no more wine at the wedding feast. Later, the church at Antioch yielded (accommodated) to the Holy Spirit when God instructed them to send Barnabas and Saul off on a missionary journey.

To be sure, the biblical events cited here are not instances where persons sought to avoid stress. However, in all three cases no action would have occurred if there had not been a need or a request for action. Obedience to the request represented one method of dealing with the stress of non-compliance. It also furthered the purposes of God.

Like avoidance, most Christian people experience accommodation every time they go about their Christian duties. It occurs when they are asked to rise to their feet in a meeting or worship service. It also occurs when they are asked to change their plans to accommodate a special meeting of their board or committee. It occurs when one individual is asked to substitute for another at the last minute and when one member of a group unwittingly makes a rude comment.

Each case cited above could at least result in an embarrassing situation, if not in an eventual fight. However, common sense tells us to acquiesce quietly to the situation in the interests of living more comfortably or helping someone else out.

Accommodation is the stance in which one person says to another, "I'll go along with you in your request or desire. You can have it your way this time." The decision may be made out of love, friendship, or the desire to please. It also may be made out of the fear of worse consequences to follow. (It may also have the effect of beginning to pile up injustices against the future, but at the moment it seems the easier way out.)

Accommodation is what the older board members did at First Church with Pastor Lyle's request for an outreach program and again at first with Pastor Bob's request. The accommodation was not processed well. It eventually resulted in negative behavior when the younger board members rallied to their pastor's defense in defiance of the older board members.

Avoidance and accommodation usually do not work well in keeping the peace and in maintaining a safe and sane environment. Because of that, the only other approach to dealing with the many stimuli that come into our lives is **confrontation.**

While confrontation is not one of the five conflict management styles studied here, it describes what three of the styles can accomplish for us. If we cannot turn our backs on a problem, or if we cannot walk alongside others and accept what they want, then we must face into the wind of adversity and interact with the problem head on.

There are three ways of confronting those issues of life that we cannot avoid or accommodate.

Competition

The most rudimentary of all confronting techniques is to compete against those problems that bother or annoy us. If the problem is disturbing enough to really "get on our nerves," tension begins to develop within us (see chapter two). It continues rising until it finally reaches the point where we are so uncomfortable that we take action to alleviate it. If we cannot avoid the issue and cannot lovingly accommodate it, then, like the shark, we instinctively try to destroy it.

Competition takes the approach, "I want to have it my way this time. In fact, I insist on having it my way. I am right and you are wrong. I have put up with enough trouble and turmoil and I intend to win this one."

Competition is not always bad but very often it reaps a whirlwind. Jacob and Esau competed without end and never were able to enjoy good family relationships. Moses killed an Egyptian who was beating a Hebrew and spent forty years in exile in the Sinai desert. Peter argued with Jesus about his need to die and Jesus rebuked him sternly. Paul and Barnabas disagreed about taking John Mark along on the second missionary journey and their team eventually had to divide.

On the more positive side, Moses brought ten plagues upon Pharaoh and as a result Pharaoh allowed Israel to leave Egypt. David withstood Goliath and eventually became the next king of Israel. Jesus rebuked demons and delivered many people who had no other hope of deliverance. The twelve apostles stood up to the Sanhedrin and the fledgling church gained great respectability in the eyes of the people of Jerusalem, including a large contingent of priests (Acts 6:7).

The difference comes in knowing when to compete, how to compete and in what manner to manage one's emotions. That will make it possible for the forces and energies within us to work for good and not for evil.

As previously mentioned, tension development is a triggering mechanism for competition. There are, in reality, three basic emotions triggered by tension development and any of them can lead to competition. They are anger, "scare," and sadness. Anger comes because of personal insult, scare comes as the result of danger and sadness is the result of loss.

When these emotions are not resolved appropriately they develop secondary emotions which intensify the conflicts. Anger turns into hate, scare becomes fear and sadness develops into depression. These secondary emotions in turn develop other complex emotional patterns which rob us of joy and effectiveness in our lives and service to Christ. They threaten our sense of contentment and well-being and rob us of the *shalom* of God. A normal and natural response to such dangers is to destroy the object of the turmoil. Seeking to do so is not sin in itself. We sin only when we take actions that inappropriately hurt other people while we are protecting ourselves. That difference is the deciding rule between appropriate and inappropriate competition.

An appropriately competitive spirit is the magic that produced leaders like Moses, David and Paul. It is also the spirit that keeps churches together in the midst of great peril and danger. It can protect people from heresy and build vast Christian empires that help many people find Christ.

An inappropriately competitive spirit can destroy churches, cripple ministries, drive people away from Christ and stifle progress in the church. The difference comes in truly knowing the mind of Christ in every situation and keeping it distinct from our own mind or viewpoint.

Compromise

Compromise is a dirty word for some people. It carries the connotation of giving in, of relaxing our standards, of accepting less than the best. In a church context it smacks of worldliness.

There is an element of risk in compromise, but it is not always a moral risk. Sometimes it is merely an ego risk.

It is not spiritually healthy for anyone to compromise his/her ethical or doctrinal standards. Neither is it psychologically healthy for anyone to compromise his/her personal commitment to being who they are. It is exceedingly important, however, to be open to new truth in every area of life. That helps us adjust our thinking, feeling and being so we may conform to the new insights that God may wish to give us.

That is why compromise can lead us to a higher plane than competition does. A competitive stance says to the opposition, "You're wrong and I'm right. That's the way it is; end of discussion." A compromising stance, on the other hand, says, "I'm not perfect in my knowledge and neither are you, but you seem to have a good idea too. Let's put part of your idea and part of mine together so we'll both have a better idea."

Esther compromised with Mordecai when he asked her to appeal to the king on behalf of the Jews. She took her life into her hands on the promise that Mordecai would provide the prayer support she needed. Daniel compromised with the king's official in testing a ten-day dietary arrangement. He said it would help him keep faith with his Jewish traditions and still not get the official into trouble.

Jesus compromised with Peter when he promised to pay the temple tax and then told him to go fishing for the money. The early church crafted a compromise agreement over circumcision that held for several years (Acts 15), keeping the church together during a time of great theological and developmental stress.

Compromise does not necessarily satisfy everyone equally, but it does allow for more variety in group life. The one drawback is that it focuses on the negative rather than on the positive. Like the crafty fox, it usually forces us to deal with the question, "What must I give up to get what I really want?" In that respect, it is a poor way to solve a problem.

Compromise is what the older members of First Church did with Pastor Bob's request for an outreach program. When they finally saw the issue would not go away, they allowed Pastor Bob and the younger members of the board to develop a plan they could put into practice. Then they reluctantly stood by and watched them struggle with it. It looked like they did not give up much, but they did give up their desire to have no plan at all. The younger members gave up their desire to have a plan everyone could accept. This was also hard for them to take. As a result some new people were added to the church, but it left an uneasy truce that erupted in a church split several years later.

There is one way that compromise could have worked better for them. The older members of the board could have agreed to a plan that would not have threatened their sense of well-being. Pastor Bob and the younger members of the board could have expressed more of a concern for the well-being of the older generation. Their hastily-devised plan gave more to the younger generation than it gave to the older generation. That added to the pile-up of injustices that later flared into serious problems for the church.

Collaboration

There is a better way to manage conflict than through the relatively more mature way of compromise. This method follows the biblical principle of placing the thoughts, ideas and feelings of others on par with our own (Phil. 2:3-4). Like the wise owl, who spends his time asking questions (Whoo-Whoo-Whoo, What, How, When, Where, Why), we seek information, not compliance.

The essence of collaboration is cooperation. In trying to join in equally with the efforts of others, the collaborating stance says, "Let's put our personal preferences aside and talk about the real underlying issues. Let's look at it from all sides until we find a solution that works best for all of us. Let's solve the problem so we can all be more fully content and grow up together in Christ." This approach makes it possible to become united in one body and brings into full flower the spirit of Christ.

Collaboration finally brings us to that point of maturity that allows us to be equally concerned for everyone. We all count equally. We all are equally important. We all matter. One does not have to give up more than is just and fair to accommodate another.

No longer do we feel the need to scheme about how much we reluctantly have to surrender to gain what someone else refuses to relinquish. We do not have to listen to persons who force their way in, threatening in blustering tones to disrupt the *shalom* of God's people just to be personally content themselves. We all finally become brothers and sisters of one another, each with a voice that will be heard.

Collaboration has great biblical precedents. Abraham and

Abimelech negotiated a treaty over their wells and Jethro and Moses talked together about how to govern Israel in the wilderness. Solomon negotiated with Hiram for timber to build the temple and Nehemiah helped the Jewish leaders decide to rebuild the temple walls. Jesus engaged Zacchaeus in a long dinner conversation that won his conversion and the elders of the early church agreed with the apostles concerning the need for seven deacons.

Collaboration calls for great maturity of spirit. We have said the most basic desire of the human being is to avoid conflict. We have also said that when conflict cannot be avoided, the most basic instinct is to compete for our own way. Because that is true, strong human emotions must be managed well for both compromise and collaboration to work.

In the case where a proposal attacks our sense of values and therefore makes us angry, compromise will lead us to bridle our anger sufficiently to be civil. Collaboration will help us rise above our anger and seek to understand the other person's viewpoint before taking offense at his/her proposal.

Sometimes a proposal attacks our sense of comfort and security, making us afraid. In such a case, compromise will lead us to ask how we may continue to protect ourselves in the face of a new situation in life. Collaboration will lead us to decide how the proposal will improve the security of our lives, though we do not see it yet.

A proposal which threatens to take away something we have long treasured, therefore making us sad, must cause us to seek an appropriate way to grieve. Compromise will allow us to keep part of that sacred treasure so we will grieve less. Collaboration will allow us to grieve honestly in the presence of our Christian family. In that way we may get beyond that point in life to newer and higher planes of joy.

Compromise would have allowed the pastors at Elm Street Church to agree that they would receive a utility allowance. Then they would have been able to pay their own utility bills without having their light bulbs monitored. Collaboration would have allowed the entire board to do a complete study of operational costs. Then they could have developed appropriate new measures for equitable cost control. Such a study would have allowed them to take into account the needs and feelings of their church servants.

At First Church, collaboration would have allowed everyone to address the deeper issue, "How can we carry out the mandate of Christ to reach the unchurched in our own Jerusalem and Judea?" It would have allowed the older members to tell their stories of a bygone day. The younger members could have said what approaches worked for them when they came into the church. Finally, the pastor could have said what he had learned about outreach strategies in seminary.

Moving beyond that, it would have allowed for some mutual sharing of grief and vision. It also would have allowed for some mutual participation in saying what they could all live with at that time in their church's history.

It may have taken several months, capped with a weekend planning retreat (see chapter twelve). Still, it surely would have worked a lot better than did the compromise and it would have developed much greater ownership within the whole church. Unrest would not have continued to fester and the pastor could have enjoyed a much longer tenure in that place of ministry.

To unify and integrate our use of all five of these conflict management styles, there are three unifying needs that must be mentioned before we end this chapter.

The Need for Spiritual Discipline

From early times men and women have sought to bring their spiritual beings into harmony with their physical and social lives. There is abundant Christian literature from the early church to the present that seeks to bring the two together.

Richard Foster has done some excellent work in collecting much of the material about the spiritual disciplines into one volume. In his 1978 bestselling book, *Celebration of Discipline*, he groups twelve spiritual disciplines under three headings, which he labels the Inner disciplines, the Outer disciplines and the Corporate disciplines. Conflict management in the church and in Christian organizations would fare much better if people practiced all twelve of these spiritual disciplines systematically.

The Need to Be Assertive

In seeking to respond positively to others who may create tensions and conflicts within us and between us, we must come to understand the difference between being aggressive, submissive and assertive.

Being aggressive is sharkish and when that approach is our first line of response it can be very destructive.

Being submissive is turtleish. As a first line of response it is not healthy either. It is good to be submissive when we know it is right to be so, but it is not good to be so by default. It robs us of our own self-identity and it robs others of the gifts we could bring into their lives.

Being assertive is owlish and should characterize our approach to life most of the time. It allows us to be fully alive, fully in control of life and fully aware of how God wants us to respond to life.

Being assertive is being straightforward in an honest and kindly manner. It avoids passive-aggressive hooks and antagonistic barbs. It is not manipulative nor complaining and it is not selfish. It simply seeks to know the truth, tell the truth and deal in truth.

The Need for a Balance of Power

Power is both absolutely necessary for getting things done and absolutely the most insidious enemy of peace in any group of people.

Power can be perceived in several ways. It is the flow of energy that motivates and drives a person forward in his/her pursuit of life. It is the defensive mechanism which causes people to lash out in protection when they feel assaulted. It is the warming element of life that draws people out of themselves to accomplish great things for good.

Power comes in small packages, large packages and many medium-sized packages. Power relates to prestige, accomplishment, insight and personality sparkle. It also relates to desire, impulse, ego and self-esteem. It relates to the way people live within themselves and to the way they live their public lives.

Whenever people gather they automatically take a reading on where they stand in the power lineup of that group. Sometimes we call it the pecking order. In a pecking order there is one person who can influence everyone in the group, one who can influence everyone minus one, another who can influence everyone minus two and so on down the line to the one who cannot influence anyone in that group.

If wholeness and *shalom* are to be a part of any Christian group of people, they must learn how to regulate their personal power. This is also true if they are to manage their conflicts well and if they are to do the will of God with a minimum amount of damage to each other. They must learn how to bring their own power level into interactive play with every other person in the group. In this way no one gets overrun by it and no one has free reign to rule as they please.

Two interactive forces also must be brought into play. Those who are stronger must actively moderate their flow of energy and drive and those who are weaker must push themselves to become stronger. Those who talk more must talk less and those who do not talk at all must learn how to gain the floor. Everyone must become a keeper of their sister and brother, so no one gets overlooked in the discussion and everyone has equal opportunity to share as they desire to share.

Sometimes an individual in the group is too shy or too strong. Then others in the group must practice assertive techniques to equalize the flow of power so the shy become strong and the strong become sensitive.

Even the best developed conflict management styles can fall prey to the absence of the three unifying needs mentioned here. You can work as hard as you will on your techniques for appropriate avoiding, accommodating and confronting. If you fail to develop your spiritual life, however, you can still fail to achieve the highest goals of *shalom*. This is also true if you fall prey to bad conversational skills at the expense of good assertive habits. Finally, if you fail to understand how to modulate your power in any group, it will certainly overwhelm some individuals.

---

1. See the bibliography for complete citations.

2. Kenneth W. Thomas and Ralph H. Kilmann, *Thomas-Kilmann Conflict Mode Instrument*, Tuxedo, New York: Xicom, 1974. See also Speed Leas, *Discover Your Conflict Management Style*, Washington, D.C.: Alban Institute, 1984 and Richard Blackburn, *How Do I Manage Differences*, Lombard Mennonite Peace Center, Lombard, Illinois, 1989.

3. I am again indebted to Norman Shawchuck, *How to Manage Conflict in the Church*, Vol. 1:22-27, for the comparisons of the five animals with which to illustrate the five conflict management styles.

PART TWO

THEOLOGY:
CONFLICT IN THE
BIBLICAL RECORD

CHAPTER FIVE

A Biblical Theology of Conflict Management

Solving Disagreements in the Church:
A Biblical Foundation

We have been moving in and out of the Scriptures in each preceding chapter. We began by hearing what James had to say about wars and quarrels among Christian people. We went on to look briefly at many examples of conflict in the biblical stories. We also took time to become acquainted with the human dynamics of conflict. Now it is time to return to the Scriptures again for a more fully developed foundation.

Several important biblical principles present themselves for our study as we seek to gain control over conflict in Christian groups and in the church so God's work may be done more effectively.

1. One is that even from a biblical perspective, *conflict is a reality in all of life*. Conflict began already in the Garden of Eden. Satan was jealous of Adam and Eve's relationship with God, so he caused Eve to desire what she did not have — the knowledge of evil and good. Satan promised she would become like God, but in coming to know evil she became more like Satan than God.

To keep humankind on the defensive against Satan after that, God said he would put enmity (conflict) between Satan and all of Eve's offspring (Gen. 3:15). The purpose for that conflict was not simply to make life more difficult for us. It was to help us defend ourselves against the wicked wiles of the devil.

God's promise was that though the serpent (i.e., Satan) would strike the heel of humankind, causing us to sin, humanity would in the end crush the head (the power) of Satan. Christ did that first on the cross, but we must continue to do it daily in our own lives through the power of the Holy Spirit.

59

Examples of the continuous conflict between Satan and humanity may be seen in the rivalry between Jacob and Esau, Moses and Miriam and David and Saul. It is also seen in the conflict between the Northern Kingdom and the Southern Kingdom in the Old Testament and between Judas Iscariot and Jesus in the New Testament.

Besides those examples, Psalm 2:1-6 speaks of the conflict between the kings of the earth and Christ. The Proverbs speak often about the tension between personal discipline and the stubborn, unyielding spirit of people (e.g., Prov. 15:32).

Isaiah also speaks of the eternal conflict we face, when he utters the words of the Lord, "Come now and let us reason together . . ." (Isa. 1:18-20). In that passage "reason" requires us to recognize our part in the sin of self-desire. Even though our sins may be red like crimson, they can be as white as snow, but the choice is up to us. God says that the outcome for obedience on our part is "eating the best of the land," while the outcome for resisting God's will is to be devoured.

2. The second principle is the need to *adopt the mind of Christ* in dealing with conflict. What is that? For one thing, Jesus taught us not to resist (contend with) an evil person (one who sins against us, Matt. 5:39). He demonstrated that by being friends with publicans and sinners. He did not condone their sin, but neither did he reject them as people. When the Pharisees criticized him, he did not answer them back sharply. Isaiah spoke of that same attitude when he said, "Even as a sheep before his shearers is dumb, so he opened not his mouth" (in evil retort, Isa. 53:7b).

Another element of the mind of Christ is to "submit to one another out of reverence for Christ" (Eph. 5:21). That Scripture stands as a final summary in answer to the question, "How should we live lives worthy of Jesus Christ?" (4:1). "Submitting to one another" refers to all believers in all situations of life. It also means paying attention to each other's ideas and needs. Finally, it includes shared decision-making.

Mutual submission to one another in Christ is a universal biblical principle of Christian behavior. It means that as we yield ourselves to one another, Christ helps us grow in our Christian lives. As we guard our tongue in a conversation we may avoid many a painful conflict in the church, in Christian organizations and in the home. This helps us listen better to each other's viewpoint and ponder it more carefully.

3. A third principle in overcoming conflict according to the mind of Christ is that we must sacrificially *put forth personal efforts to make peace.* Jesus said peace**makers** are blessed, not peace lovers. Paul urges us to "make every effort to keep the unity of the Spirit through the bond of peace" (Eph. 4:3).

We can do that by seeking the Spirit's power to "live in harmony with one another" (Rom. 12:21a).

Living in harmony means we share our ideas with one another, talking things over rather than resisting another person's viewpoint. "Talking things over" happens best by listening carefully to each other, even when there are disagreements. Sometimes it is helpful to list all the ideas that everyone has on a piece of paper or on a marker board. Then we can use that list to seek a solution that will meet as many of the people's needs as possible.

"Not being overcome by evil" means when something evil (e.g., a temptation) or an evil person threatens to overwhelm us, we use God's strength within us to resist and withstand that evil without sinning in response.

Another way of making peace is by putting others first. Philippians 2:3-4 tells us to "do nothing out of selfish ambition or vain conceit, but in humility consider others better than yourselves. . . . Look not only to your own interests, but also to the interests of others." Jesus often did that. Think of the time he sent Peter out to catch a fish so he could pay the temple tax and avoid embarrassment for Peter (Matt. 17:24-27). It is amazing how many quarrels we can avoid by recognizing that our brother or sister has a right to his/her own ideas also. We cannot always have everything the way we like it. We must learn to respect the opinions of others.

Finally, we must learn how to use the biblical steps of reconciliation better. We find them in Matthew 18:15-20. We discussed this passage briefly in chapter three, but here we wish to expand on it.

Step One is to talk personally to the other party. In that conversation we must share our sense of hurt and offense, rather than making demands for them to change. We must let them come to understand how we feel, so they can truly desire to make right what needs to be changed.

If that does not produce good results, Step Two is next. Here we take a few others with us for a second conversation. The purpose for the others going along is not to bolster "our own side" but to secure impartial mediation. In our day and age, that may refer to one or two deacons, the pastor, a spiritual friend, or a neutral, outside, third-party mediation team.

The Third Step moves beyond mediation to arbitration. If the offender does not reconcile in Step Two, we may "tell it to the church." In today's context, "the church" could be represented by the church council, the elders, the deacons, the pastoral relations committee, or another committee with authority to give direction. The representatives of the church should listen prayerfully and humbly to both sides and then render a decision based on their best judgment. Because this text deals with personal disputes rather than with whole church issues, the church cannot enforce compliance, however.

Verse 17, "let him/her be to you as a sinner or a tax collector," does not necessarily require excommunication, separation, divorce, resignation, or firing. It does require love and spiritual care. Sinners and tax collectors were people Jesus sought to win back to God. He never rejected one of them, although they sometimes rejected him. Perhaps if there were a greater spirit of Christian caring in today's world and less judging, there would not be so much hurting. Acting in such an accepting manner requires bigness of heart, manifesting the kind of compassion that Jesus often exemplified.

Verses 19-20, "where two or three of you are gathered in my name," points out that united, dedicated prayer has great power in bringing about a positive answer. In other words, God can answer any prayer for conflict resolution that you decide to pray, if you pray it together. If the church would pray together more when they have a dispute over anything (including a program, the pastor, a remodeling program, or any other tension), there would be less tearing apart. It is important, however, to pray for a common acceptable solution, rather than praying that "the other side" will see it your way.

Solving Disagreements Among God's Chosen People: Biblical Examples

First Corinthians 10:1-13 provides an important paradigm for understanding how to apply the biblical materials pertaining to conflict. In speaking about the experiences of the Israelites in the wilderness, Paul asserts:

These things happened to them as examples and were written down as warnings for us, on whom the fulfillment of the ages has come.

So, if you think you are standing firm, be careful that you don't fall (10:6)!

In this text ancient Israel serves as a mirror for us, showing the result of both good and bad behavior. Verses one to five show that spiritual food and spiritual drink were available for all the people in ancient Israel. Yet some of them misappropriated those resources and did not receive the spiritual food and drink that God made available to them. Those who did receive it benefitted by it, but those who did not receive it experienced great loss.

In verses six to ten we encounter four examples of how people did not benefit by the spiritual food and drink that God offered to them. This resulted in dire consequences for them and four stern warnings for us. They include not worshipping pagan gods like some of the people did, not sinning sexually like some did who died because of it, not stretching God's patience like some of the people did who then were bitten by snakes and finally, not grumbling like some of them did who died as a result.

The principle here is that God expects us to learn from the experiences of other people. It is especially important in relation to mistakes and failures that we give attention to God's warnings in the scriptures. Such warnings are applicable to other areas of life besides the four mentioned above, including destructive conflict.

Everyone experiences differences of opinion with others at some point in their lives. Sometimes husbands and wives do not agree on all the details in their relationship. At times brothers and sisters cannot agree on how to play or what TV programs to watch. Sometimes mothers and daughters or fathers and sons or other combinations of family members see things quite differently and clash as a result.

There are times when people in families, groups, churches, businesses, clubs and community organizations have different points of view about issues facing them. How they handle those differences is extremely important for life to flow positively, happily and smoothly. Those who do not experience a successful resolution of conflict will encounter the pain, problems and struggles which conflict brings in their lives. Those who do find the right way to resolve their differences and to settle their disputes in life will experience the gracious and bounteous blessing of God.

The third section of this text, (verses 11-13), show that people are never so strong that they may not fail again. Let him/her who thinks s/he stands be careful of that, Scripture says. Just because one was strong yesterday does not mean s/he will be safe tomorrow. It is important, therefore, to be constantly on guard. People must continuously renew their spiritual food and drink, continuously remind themselves of the principles taught by the Lord and continuously avail themselves of the strength God offers.

Happily, the good news is that even when temptations come, God's strength and power is always sufficient for us. God will not allow us to be tempted beyond our ability to withstand. He will give us the strength and the courage we need to face the conflict. When we fall and we will, he will forgive us, strengthen us and help us do better again.

In this context we can freely examine the conflicts reported in Scripture and seek the lessons they teach us about conflict resolution.[1]

As we pointed out in chapter one, there are more than 133 occasions when people disagreed with each other in Scripture. The first one is Adam and Eve's decision to eat the forbidden fruit. The last one is the apostles' need to deal with false prophets in 2 Peter, Jude and 2 and 3 John. All the disagreements can be classified according to the five conflict management styles we discussed in chapter four. They also can be evaluated in terms of how successful each style was in accomplishing the intention of the respondent.[2]

Avoidance

The first of the five conflict management styles we will review is avoidance. It occurs three times in the Bible. That may come as a surprise, until we remember that the Bible is a dynamic collection of literature. People were always acting on behalf of causes or for the preservation of life. In all three cases of avoidance it was the appropriate way to resolve the problem that people encountered. In all three cases the outcome was positive.

We find the first one in Genesis 39. Joseph was already living in Potipher's house where he experienced the seductive advances of Potipher's wife. Knowing he would be unable to successfully manage that conflict any other way, he just left. In fact, he ran out of the house. It is true that he spent two years in jail as a result, but in the end he was promoted and eventually became the prime minister of Egypt.

The second case of avoidance is in 1 Samuel 19-26, the ongoing saga of how King Saul tried repeatedly to kill David. David could not handle that one any other way. He knew if he tried to fight back he would throw the nation into civil war and he did not think that would be right. So he simply kept avoiding Saul's military presence. He kept fleeing, escaping, hiding and waiting until God's timing was right. Finally, when Saul died, David was elected to take his place.

The third case is in Luke 9:51-56, where Jesus passed through Samaria on his way to Jerusalem with his disciples. People of Samaria did not look kindly upon Jews who traveled to Jerusalem to worship. They believed Mount Gerazim was where God ought to be worshipped. That belief stemmed from the fact that Mount Gerazim was the first site for the worship of God after the Israelites occupied Palestine under Joshua (Deut. 27:12-13; c.f. Josh. 24:1).

When the two disciples entered a village of Samaria the "No vacancy" signs went up. Two of the disciples wanted to call down fire from heaven like Elijah had done in the Old Testament. However, Jesus' response was to go on down the road in search of another place to lodge for the night. It was an appropriate use of the avoidance style of conflict management.

Accommodation

Accommodation occurs nineteen times in the Bible. Only twice does it result in a negative outcome. Seventeen times it has positive results. The two negative examples occur in Genesis 3 and John 9. In Genesis 3 Adam accommodated Eve in her desire to eat the fruit of the forbidden tree, with devastating results.

In John 9 the man who was born blind and had his eyes opened by Jesus told the Pharisees, in good faith, who had healed him. Unfortunately, the Pharisees turned his honesty against him, expelling him from the synagogue. He did the right thing, but the Pharisees brought pain upon him and caused a fracture in the synagogue family. Sometimes that is the price people pay for doing what they believe is right.

However, there are many other times when accommodation worked well. We find two graphic examples in Genesis 3 and in 2 Samuel 12. In Genesis 3 Adam and Eve became convicted of their sin and confessed it to God. When God called out to them they came forward and confessed their wrong instead of running away. They agreed with God, accepted, or accommodated his verdict and consequently received his forgiveness. Though they had to leave the garden as a punishment for their sin they did not have to leave God's family. God's forgiveness made it possible for them to stay in relationship with him.

We find the second example of a positive outcome in 2 Samuel 12. Nathan, the prophet, came to David and accused him of sinning with Bathsheba. The king could have banished the prophet from town, but instead he humbled himself, admitted his sin and repented of it. As a result he was able to rise above those dismal circumstances and continue to serve the Lord.

Competition

Competition occurs more frequently in the Bible than any other conflict management style. A total of sixty-five occurrences of competition may be found. There were times in the Bible when this method was appropriate and worked well. That is true for a total of sixteen times.

One example where competition worked well is in Genesis 37, 42 and 45. This is the story of the quarrel between Joseph and his brothers. Joseph had some dreams that his brothers did not like. They threw him into a hole and then sold him to some traveling salesmen. The salesmen in turn took him to Egypt and sold him again.

Some years later the brothers came to Egypt to buy food, but because of their earlier behavior Joseph decided to test them by putting them in jail (competitive behavior). However, after they had learned their lesson Joseph offered to make peace with them. He brought his entire family to Egypt from Canaan and fed them during a very long famine. A competitive style of sibling rivalry started out badly but ended up producing great good in the long term.

The second example is in Matthew 4:1-11, where we read of the devil's temptation of Jesus. Jesus demonstrated the competitive approach in his three rebuttals, begun each time with the words, "It is written." Finally he said, "Get thee behind me, Satan. You shall not tempt the Lord your God."

In Joseph's case he needed to stand up and tell his brothers that they had wronged him before they could work out their differences. In Jesus' case he needed to tell the devil that he (Satan) was on the wrong side and that Jesus would not give in to those temptations. Clearly in these two cases as in the fourteen others, it was necessary to stand up for what was right.

On the other hand, there are forty-nine times in the Bible when the competitive approach did not result in a good solution. Some of the most painful encounters between people in the Bible occurred when they tried to solve their problems competitively. Let us look briefly at five examples. The first one is in Genesis 25, 27 and 33. The ongoing quarrels between Jacob and Esau strained their relationship so greatly that they never were able to live side by side in the same land.

The second example relates closely to that same family. We find it in Genesis 29 and 30. It tells of the sibling rivalry of two sisters, Leah and Rachel. We do not know how they got along before they met Jacob, but after they met him things did not work out too well for them. After they had both married him they were in competition against each other for Jacob's favor for the rest of their lives, never really establishing peaceful relations again.

We find the third example in the four gospels. Throughout the ministry of Jesus, he and the Pharisees clashed. There was only one exception to that rule and that was in Jesus' encounter with Nicodemus. Nicodemus was open to the new truth that Jesus brought to him while the other Pharisees were not. The results of those clashes produced a terrible fracture in the Jewish community as the Pharisees kept opposing the teachings of Jesus.

The fourth example is even more painful. In Acts 5 Ananias and Sapphira came to the church individually with their offerings. Peter suspected there was a problem and asked them to tell the full truth. They stubbornly persisted in telling a lie and as a result they suffered death at the hand of God.

The fifth example is also sad. In Acts 15:36-41 Paul and Barnabas decided to revisit the churches they had founded earlier. This occurred after a very successful first missionary journey, followed by a gratifying conference at which church unity was restored.

As they discussed their plans for a second missionary journey, Barnabas said he wanted to give John Mark another chance, but Paul refused. Clearly both had good arguments. However, both stayed on the "Yes" and "No" treadmill until they finally separated. Barnabas went in one direction and Paul went another way. We may rationalize by saying it must have been God's will, for he greatly blessed their efforts. Yet the sad fact is that two genuine, loving and important Christian leaders parted company for the wrong reasons.

Compromise

Compromise occurs four times in the Bible and all four of them come out on the positive side. Here we will look at two examples. In Daniel 1, Daniel and his three friends asked the king's official for a ten–day dietary test. In effect, they wanted to make a compromise with the official and it worked. As a result they avoided a very ugly fight.

In Acts 15 some very strict Jewish Christians wanted all the Gentile Christians in Antioch to obey the Law of Moses in addition to Jesus' teachings. The Greek converts, on the other hand, felt it did not make sense to have to submit to circumcision, obey all the food laws and accept all the other things that were merely Jewish customs.

The two sides could not agree on a solution by themselves, so they went down to Jerusalem for a mediation conference. At that conference they struck a bargain. James, the leading elder of the church, summarized the agreement by suggesting the Gentiles should submit only to four things. They agreed to this bargain, a compromise and it worked for several years. It healed the church and kept them together as one.

Collaboration

Collaboration occurs twenty times in Scripture, seventeen of which are positive. One of the three examples that did not work well is that of Moses, who tried to resolve a difficult dispute with Korah (Num. 16). In that instance Korah and 250 other priests felt that Moses had too much power.

Moses prayed, pled and tried to negotiate with Korah to settle the dispute amicably. He even offered to let the Lord settle the matter for both of them. Korah, on the other hand, remained adamant, refusing to enter into collaboration with Moses. The result was that the earth opened up and swallowed Korah and his friends. No one ever saw them again.

The examples of how collaboration worked positively far outnumber the negative. In the book of Ruth, Naomi went off to a far country with her family but came back as a widow, bringing her daughter-in-law Ruth back with her. Because Ruth cooperated (collaborated) with Naomi they were able to find a good husband for her. Ruth's benefit from her collaboration with Naomi included a happy home, a stable marriage and a stable family. Ultimately it also provided Ruth the opportunity of becoming the great-grandmother of King David.

Another example of how collaboration works is in Acts 6. Some widows in the church thought they were getting cheated in the daily distribution of food. When grumbling erupted, the apostles called a meeting of the leading elders of the church. The apostles presented the problem to them with a possible solution. We may assume that the entire group discussed the pros and cons of the issue until they found a solution suitable to the whole group. The result was that they selected seven deacons to help care for the expanding needs of the church.

A review of the score card presented in this study quickly suggests that competition is the least effective way to resolve differences. Putting aside those conflicts with mixed results, collaboration and accommodation are by far the strongest and best ways to resolve conflict.

As long as a person chooses any one of the styles at the right time and uses them in the right way, they all work. Some are more effective for developing friendships and establishing relationships and some are more effective in encountering strong temptations or evil influences. The ultimate value of each is not in using any one of them arbitrarily, but in using all of them prudently and at the right time.

STYLE	POSITIVE	NEGATIVE
Avoidance	03	00
Accommodation	17	02
Competition	16	49
Compromise	04	00
Collaboration	17	03
TOTALS	57	54

It is important to understand the practical biblical lessons we can glean from Scripture about conflict management. It is also important, however, to understand the three basic doctrinal statements in the Bible concerning the issue of resolving differences between people.

The first statement concerns the importance of obeying God's rules (a competitive stance). The Ten Commandments are based on respecting God and other people in their basic rights. This includes the right to life, truth, parental respect, family integrity, security of possessions and freedom from jealous neighbors. In other words, the right way to solve conflicts about basic human rights is to respect other people's rights whether you agree with them or not.

The second principle comes from Romans 14 and 15. Those who are stronger in Christ must learn to be patient with those who are weaker (an accommodating stance). The application for conflict management is that some people cannot handle conflict as well as others. One who is strong must be strong enough to overlook a weaker person's foibles and follies for the sake of peace and harmony in the family of Christ.

If the issue in dispute is not one of basic human rights, it is likely that it is not serious enough to risk doing damage to the Christian family. Even if it is one of basic rights, it may be better to suspend those rights temporarily for the sake of the other person's Christian growth and development.

The third principle is in Romans 12:9-21. Simply put, sincere love overcomes all obstacles (a collaborative stance). There is nothing more important in life than to love other members in the Christian family. We are not speaking here of the romantic, feeling type of love which is glorified by our culture today. Rather, true Christian love is a basic deep-seated caring about the needs of others. When other persons make mistakes, we continue to care about them anyway, looking for ways to help them make their life better. We continue to care for them even when their mistakes have negative consequences for us. After all, godly love overcomes all obstacles. There is no room for excuses concerning that principle.

When I taught at a Christian high school in Oklahoma we had a superintendent with whom some faculty members did not always agree. As I sat in faculty meetings week after week I often thought to myself, "Wouldn't it be good if we could talk openly, honestly and objectively about the issues, rather than merely defending our own feelings in any matter?"

It would have been so good if we could have separated our feelings from the objective facts pertinent to the various issues. That way we could have come to fairer, more honest and more caring solutions that would have benefitted everyone. That is the substance of God's highest good for his believing family. That is the goal for which he wants us all to strive daily.

---

1. Marlin E. Thomas, *A Study of Conflict in the Bible*, Colorado Springs, Colo.: Resources for Resolving Life's Issues, 1988.

2. In this section we define conflict management styles from the standpoint of one who was forced to defend him/herself in a conflict, not from the standpoint of the one who presented the problem.

CHAPTER SIX

Profiles of Problem Solving in the Early Church

It is dangerous to turn any one of the Bible's stories into a categorical statement of absolute doctrine. It is better to take the approach we find in 1 Corinthians 10. That chapter presents biblical stories as examples of what worked and what did not work in the lives of God's people.

In this chapter we will review the leadership styles of Moses, Joshua, Samuel, the kings of Israel and the apostle Paul. These will help us understand biblical approaches to conflict management and problem solving. These are not the only models available in the Bible. However, they do give us some perspective on how different persons addressed a variety of issues in the emerging nation of Israel.

Following a study of Old Testament leadership styles we will review the struggle of the early church as it looked for leadership models that met the needs it encountered.

We will soon see that there is no "best" leadership style in the Bible. Neither is there only one "New Testament model." God's leaders adapted their leadership styles to suit the needs they encountered.

Jesus Christ never wrote a church constitution. He left that up to the creativity of the Holy Spirit working within the body of the church. In that way the many needs of God's people in many different ages could be met better without undue tensions or technical organizational debates.

Because of that, we should not view church constitutions today as permanently fixed entities for regulating church government. They are only temporary tools to help us do God's work better. When the needs change, the tools change. Blessed is the church that is able to revise its constitution without pain as often as the needs of its people change and without binding the Spirit of the Lord.

Background: Old Testament Models of Leadership

By modern standards, Moses used a competitive model of leadership. Willard Claassen would have called him a benevolent dictator.[1] The competitive style of leadership was "in his blood" already early in his life. He tried to settle a quarrel between an Egyptian supervisor and a Hebrew slave in that manner (Exod. 2:11-14). However, he was also able to temper his bombastic approach in the years that followed. As a result he became a much more effective leader.

His approach to leadership was what God needed to move the Hebrew people from Egypt to Canaan and forge them into a tribal nation. When he met with the elders of the people in Exodus 4:29-31 he simply presented them with the miraculous evidences of God's call and they believed. Subsequently, as Pharaoh's heart progressively hardened, they required more and more persuasion to keep from weakening.

Pharaoh was harder to convince. The signs of Moses did not affect him nor did Moses' authoritative stance make any difference to Pharaoh. It took ten plagues to bring about a reluctant change of heart within him. As we study the ten plagues, we can quickly see that Moses used many other persuasive measures first. He also interspersed each plague with another opportunity for repentance and cooperation.

In the wilderness Moses tempered his strong leadership style with meekness. His style of meekness should not be mistaken for weakness. It was the style of a man who had learned to care deeply for the people with whom he worked. He preferred to call forth the good in others rather than demand compliance. However, when compliance was appropriate, Moses exacted it of the people in the name of God.

Joshua was competitive as a military leader but collaborative in his domestic policy. No internal factions dared question his military leadership and no Canaanite coalition of kings received any mercy. However, he was much more mellow in his dealings with his own fellow citizens.

He listened attentively to the elders of the Trans-Jordanian tribes — Rueben, Gad and Manasseh-west — as they requested permission to let their families stay on the eastern side of Jordan. When he heard them promise to fight alongside their brothers until they conquered the whole land he willingly struck a deal with them. He was even open to collaboration with

Canaanite strangers, negotiating a treaty with the Gibeonites that provided leniency for them in spite of their treachery.

He cast lots when Achan sinned to be sure the verdict fell on the right man. After they won the land he allowed the elders of Israel to apportion the land to each tribe. Then, after they had duly assigned the land to each tribe, Joshua retired to his allotted holdings. He let the designated leaders of each tribal group govern the internal affairs of their tribe.

When it was time for Joshua to pass from this life, he summoned all the elders, leaders, judges and officials of Israel for his farewell speech (Josh. 23:1-2 and 24:1). He gave his challenge to them open-endedly and they received it freely. He placed no monarchical demands upon them. He only presented the moral obligation to revere God who had given them the land.

The Scriptures are thus able to record that Israel followed the Lord throughout the lifetime of Joshua and the elders who survived him. This shows that although Joshua did not rule autocratically, his influence continued to be felt and followed for as long as the leaders of his generation lived.

Fully two centuries later Samuel inherited a loose federation of tribes that routinely governed their own internal affairs. They only looked to the capable charismatic qualities of a national figure for national security and religious solidarity.

It is clear from the record in 1 Samuel that Samuel was trained in the prevailing style of leadership for presiding religious figures. It appears he did not have a desire to achieve political or military superiority over other leaders or nations. This was a comfortable way for him to live and it allowed the tribal federation ample freedom to follow the traditional format of home rule. However, it did not provide an effective method for dealing with the external threat of the Philistines.

We can clearly see the ineptness of the collaborative style of leadership for purposes of national defence in 1 Samuel 7. For twenty years the ark had been in exile and for twenty years the Philistines had maintained passive superiority over the Israelites. Finally Samuel called for a holy war against the passive, de facto aggressors when he assembled all Israel at Mizpah. A great victory for the Israelite militia followed, which both heartened Israel and greatly annoyed the Philistines. However, it was not long afterward that the Israelite leadership asked for a king to lead them as Samuel was not consistently effective in foreign policy.

Samuel's leadership style in selecting the first king of Israel was definitely collaborative. It was at the prompting of the elders of Israel that he began to talk with the Lord about selecting a king (chap. 8) and it was to the council of elders that Samuel first brought his candidate (9:22-24).

Only after that meal, where we may assume the elders gave their endorsement of the candidate, did Samuel anoint Saul as the official candidate for king. The later lottery at Mizpah (10:17-18) served as a system of checks and balances so the people could see that their leaders were following the will of God.

Samuel continued to exercise moral and religious leadership long after Saul began to reign, although in his usual collaborative style he did not demand the limelight. He sought to lead the militia in its usual mandated prayers before any battle (chap. 13) and sought to advise the king regarding God's will in foreign affairs (chap. 15). However, after Saul soundly rejected his advice, Samuel retired from active leadership. He returned only once to anoint David, the future second king of Israel.

The development of leadership styles reached its zenith under Samuel. Kingship did nothing to enhance or refine leadership; if anything it caused a retrenchment. It was characteristic for kings who needed legitimization to seek the advice and support of the ruling elders or priests of Israel/Judah. However, all too often that collaboration got set aside as the kings gained power.

Saul's leadership style is hard to judge, for he served more as a military commander in charge of foreign affairs than as a ruling monarch. His militia first engaged the Ammonites, then the Philistines and then the Amalekites. During the rest of his reign he continued to fight with the Philistines and pursue David.

David displayed a greater ability to relate to the elders of Israel than Saul did. He already had developed a communication network with local civilian leaders during his years of outlawry from Saul. That network continued to grow during his seven-year reign in Hebron. His elevation to Jerusalem came at the request of the elders of Israel. However, as he became more solidly entrenched, his circle of advisors shifted more to his royal court. There is less and less mention of the elders of Israel in later accounts of his kingship.

Solomon received the authority to rule from his father David, not from the elders of Israel. It seems throughout his reign Solomon ruled as a powerful monarch, consulting primarily with his own professional court advisors. Toward the end of his reign there is evidence that the people groaned under the heavy yoke he placed upon them and had very little recourse or redress of grievances.

The Scriptures make no mention at all of Rehoboam consulting with the elders of Israel. His advisors were young men of the court, very likely friends with whom he had grown up. Following his reign there is virtually no mention of any constructive relationship between the ruling class and those whom they governed. The monarchical leadership style seemed more and more to be that of competition, of autocratic direction handed down from the court. Sometimes it was more benevolent than at other times, but under the kings the people and their elders really had very little to say about their futures.

The Early Church

The era of the first century A.D. saw the eldership style of leadership in place again among the Jews. After the Exile, Zerubbabel had tried to establish a dynasty with little success. Ezra had redeveloped the elder system in Judea as it had flourished in Babylon and it slowly took root.

The Hasmoneans (led by the Maccabees) had maintained their own dynasty for a century (167-67 B.C.) but it did not last either. When Jesus came on the scene there were two types of leadership in place. One was the council of local elders in each village. The other was the ruling class of the priests, epitomized in the Council of Seventy, also known as the Sanhedrin.

Acts 1:12-26. The first leadership meetings

Jesus formed the church on Easter evening when he met with the disciples and breathed on them, giving them the Holy Spirit (John 20:22). However, Jesus instructed them to wait in Jerusalem until they had received power from the Holy Spirit (Acts 1:8) before pursuing church growth and development. For the next ten days they did just that, gathering frequently for prayer. Soon the group had grown to 120. As they prayed, it became apparent that Judas Iscariot should be replaced. There was no precedent for anyone taking over the leadership, except in the leadership style with which they were familiar. Jesus had assumed a prophetic leadership style while he was with them, so it was natural that one of them would do the same. The one who first became their spokesperson was Peter, whose name always stands first in the gospels in the lists of the disciples.

The phrase in verse 23, "so they proposed," suggests that the group in the upper room naturally fell into the discussion style of the synagogue. In that style a ruling elder led the discussion and other leading men of the group participated. The election was held by lot, which also was a part of their tradition and the outcome was acceptable to everyone.

Acts 2:36-47. The first weeks of the church

When the power of the Holy Spirit impelled the group out into the streets, all 120 apparently witnessed publicly concerning the resurrection of Christ. However, when the uproar reached mob proportions, Peter again became the spokesperson for the group and defended their actions. When spiritual conviction came upon the people and they asked various apostles what they should do, Peter voiced the answer for them all.

The days that followed were filled with joy and growth, as people sought out the apostles each day in the temple courts and fellowshipped together in their homes. There was absolutely no organization, for while the apostles provided the teaching in true rabbinical style, the people themselves took care of each other's needs. Fellowship and breaking of bread was spontaneous, not needing the guidance of approved leaders or the development of a constitution.

Acts 5:41-6:7. The first year of the church

The first year of the early church went by almost unheralded in organizational history. There is a long story of how Peter and John healed a lame man on their way to prayer and how that brought about the conversion of many people. There is also the story of how Barnabas sold a field and brought the proceeds to the apostles for distribution to the poor and how Ananias and Sapphira conspired to secretly keep part of their proceeds back when they made their gift. That is followed by an account of how the apostles were persecuted by the Sanhedrin for their public preaching.

The statement which follows the account of that persecution leads into the story of how the first seven deacons were selected and that is important for our study. The statement in Acts 5:42

shows that in spite of setbacks and persecution the apostles continued preaching and teaching the good news about Jesus.

It was in this course of events that some of the additional work they had taken on began to slip. Their joint responsibilities of preaching/teaching and administering benevolent funds became so great that they finally had to ask for help. Although Acts 6:2 indicates that the Twelve gathered "all the believers" together, the statement must be taken to be representative. It would have been impossible to assemble more than 5,000 believers for this discussion.

The way in which the Twelve went about solving this problem is instructive for conducting the business of the church. There was no eldership in place, as there was in Jewry, although it is not hard to imagine that some levels of gifted leadership had already begun to emerge. It was to this representative body of believers that the apostles presented their problem.

After laying out the problem and recommending a possible solution, the apostles allowed the group to process the recommendation and make a response. According to Acts 6:5 the recommendation was acceptable to the group, which then proceeded to make the seven appointments. This is the first recorded instance of group decision-making in the early church after Pentecost and it appears it came as close to true collaboration as any decision-making in the entire first century era.

Acts 15:1-23. After the first twenty years of the church

The scripture says little more about *bona fide* church organizational polity for the next twenty years or so. There are several stories about continued outreach and church planting. In those stories the apostle or lay leader (Philip in Acts 8) responsible for the mission was the sole director thereof.

At times there was some collaboration. Two examples are the apostles sending Peter and John to Samaria and Peter explaining his actions in Cornelius' house to the believers in Jerusalem (Acts 11).

The next major exercise in church group leadership comes in Acts 15. The church in Antioch had a major dispute with conservative delegates from Jerusalem over traditional Jewish practices. It could not be resolved in Antioch, so the believers of Antioch decided to refer the matter to a higher court. It is clear from verses four and six that by this time at least a two-tiered decision-making structure had developed. The whole church, led by the apostles and the elders, extended the welcome to them. Then later, when the debate got underway, the meeting involved the principal participants and the apostles and elders.

Tradition suggests that at least eight of the apostles were no longer in Jerusalem at the time of this conference. James, the son of Zebedee, was dead (Acts 12:2) and Thomas was already in India. Some apostles were working in Syria, Persia, Armenia and other regions by this time.[2] Therefore, the few who were still in Jerusalem served primarily as consultants and advisors to the elders, who provided the actual oversight and direction in the affairs of the church.

The person who finally summarized the consensus of the discussion was James, the brother of Jesus. He is generally accepted as the presiding elder of the church in Jerusalem.

This decision was not really the result of a full and complete consensus. That is evident by the fact that some Judaizing persons continued to dog the footsteps of Paul. In addition, Paul finally broke with the decision regarding food offered to idols (1 Cor. 8). In spite of that, this conference decision was a real departure from the way people in the biblical world made decisions. It was very much in line with Jesus' teaching in Matthew 20:25-27.

Acts 20:17,25-32; 1 Timothy 1:3-7; Revelation 2:1-7. The Ephesus connection, A.D. 5-45 in Ephesus

Paul, assisted by Aquila and Priscilla, planted the church in Ephesus. Paul, as the founding missionary, was its first leader. However, he was there for only three years and before he left, Aquila and Priscilla had probably already returned to Rome.

As usual, however, Paul did not leave the church without leadership. When he stopped at Miletus for a brief visit several months after leaving Ephesus (Acts 20:17), he called for the elders of the church and visited briefly with them.

During that visit it became apparent that Paul had passed the baton of leadership to the lay elders. He encouraged them to fulfill the role both of organizational leaders and pastors. Their chief responsibilities included keeping heresy out of the church and nurturing the flock in the way of Christ. Paul's farewell to them shows they were good friends of his and he trusted them with carrying out the work of God in their city.

Paul fully expected his life to end when he arrived in Jerusalem. That did not happen, however, so he was able to continue his relationship with Ephesus and also with his other churches. After an imprisonment of two years in Caesarea and two more years in Rome, he was able to travel again. One of the places he visited was Ephesus. Before that visit, however, he had written a letter to the church during his imprisonment in Rome.

There is no hint in the letter to Ephesus of any leadership structures at work in the church. However, 1 Timothy tells us a lot about Paul's charismatic leadership style in all his churches.

Evidently when Paul arrived in Ephesus after his Roman release, he found things were not going so well there. He promptly installed Timothy as a special care pastor in the church to put things in order again (1 Tim. 1:3-4).

Later, in his letter to Timothy written from Macedonia, he discussed that problem and the need for clear moral guidelines for bishops (elders) and deacons. Evidently it did not bother the founding pastor of the church to do whatever he needed to do to keep the church moving in the right direction.

Not long after Paul's intervention in Ephesus his life did come to an end. Timothy moved on to other endeavors and the apostle John relocated to Ephesus. John became its chief resident pastor until his retirement some twenty years later (ca. A.D. 85).

A decade after that, when John wrote the Apocalypse (ca. A.D. 95), he addressed the first of the seven letters to the churches in Ephesus (Rev. 2-3). Verse two of chapter two shows that Ephesus was back on track again, this time able to detect false apostles and keep them from influencing the church. Evidently the lay leadership of the church was in better shape by then.

Hebrews 2:1-4; 3:12-13; 5:11-6:3; 10:19-25,32-36; 12:7-15. The Roman connection, from year A.D. 20

Although the authorship of the book of Hebrews is anonymous, its destination is not so cloudy. Some elements of the book suggest that its primary audience was to the Jewish Christians in Rome.

The tone of the book shows that the readers were struggling with tensions between the Law and the new way of Christ. The purpose of the book was to call them back to renewed faithfulness to Jesus after their initial enthusiasm had encountered repeated waves of disbelief and persecution.

The Roman church began quite differently from other Mediterranean churches, in that no missionary apostle first traveled there to preach the gospel. Acts 2:10-11 shows that both Roman Jews and proselytes were visiting in Jerusalem on the Day of Pentecost when the church was born. They undoubtedly carried the gospel back to Rome and slowly a new church emerged.

The Hebrew church in Rome, composed primarily of Jews, evidently grew up from the grass roots, out of its own spiritual life. It maintained itself for at least two decades before beginning to waver.

In A.D. 49 Claudius evicted many Jews from Rome, no doubt including many Christian Jews. That hardship, along with other current issues, called for a letter of encouragement. Thus an anonymous Jewish leader of the early church wrote to encourage the believers in the capital city of Rome to remain firm and faithful to Christ. The author was likely of Hebrew background, especially in light of the words "our" in 1:1 and "we" in 2:1, among other references.

Most of the references cited above show a strong fraternal relationship between the believers of the Roman church. There is hardly a trace of paternalism in evidence, as we sometimes find in Paul's address to his "children."

The phrase used in 2:1 is "we must pay more careful attention," and in 3:12-13 the admonition is "see to it, brothers" and "encourage one another daily." In 6:1 it is "let us leave the elementary teachings . . . and go on to maturity," and in 10:23 it is "let us hold unswervingly to the hope."

The strongest hint of all concerning the structural style of leadership in the Roman church appears at this point. Verse 24 encourages the believers to "spur one another on" and verse 25 adds, "let us not give up meeting together." That is markedly different from Paul's style of address when members of his churches had problems.

Hebrews 12:7-12 does depart from the more prominent collegial style of leadership, showing that the author is "apart from" as well as "part of." Still, it is not strong enough to destroy the evidence for a "brotherhood" as opposed to a more traditional eldership model of leadership.

A Summary of Leadership Styles

A Prophetic Leadership Style

Moses offers the first example of corporate religious leadership in the Bible. His (competitive) prophetic style when he encountered Pharaoh and when he confronted the variety of problems in the wilderness was well suited to the needs of his people. God's objectives for Israel could not have been accomplished by any other leadership style.

Moses received his instructions from God, delivered them to the people and led them forth to overcome their obstacles. Because of his undaunting, fearless approach, the people of Israel were successful in making the transition from slavery to nationhood.

A Charismatic Leadership Style

Joshua's charismatic style made it possible for him to be flexible. He was firm in leading his troops so they won their battles. Yet he worked with his elders and tribal leaders so the people could express their own interests and ideas and care for their own domestic needs.

He was able to focus the issue when they lost the first battle of Ai. He was also able to deal with the problem of sin in such a way as to preserve the integrity and identity of God's people. He was God's man for bridging the gap between a wandering people and an established people.

A Collaborative Leadership Style

Samuel was neither prophetic nor charismatic in his leadership style. He was a devoted religious leader and a judge, riding his circuit regularly between three towns in central Ephraim.

When the Philistine presence pressed upon the land too heavily, he assembled the Israelite militia at Mizpah. He led them by using religious ritual, not by the powerful presence of a kingly personage. He led the people in their selection of Saul as the first king, but did nothing without the collaboration of the elders of the people.

He privately anointed David, but that was at the specific and direct command of God. Later he brought God's word to King Saul concerning the Amalekites, but only grieved that Saul did not cooperate with him in fully executing the will of God. He took no authoritative, corrective action.

Samuel was the right kind of leader for a settled people. However, he did not do well in helping them through their national crises or in managing the political changes that came into their lives.

His collaborative style even followed him in death. When he was called back from the dead to meet with Saul (1 Sam. 28), he simply stated there was nothing more to say. A prophetic type of leader would at least have delivered a redemptive oration aimed at moving the hearer to repentance.

An Autocratic Leadership Style

The kings of Judah and Israel were neither prophetic nor charismatic nor collaborative in their leadership styles. They followed the policies of the kings of the nations around them, commanding their armies, raising taxes and building empires as their desires and expediency dictated.

Some of them collaborated with their people better than others, but none of them were really sensitive first to the expressed needs of their people. They did what seemed best in their own eyes to further their causes and to protect their national interests.

An Eldership Leadership Style

The general leadership style of the early church was the same as the Jewish communities out of which it came. In the election of Matthias, in the selection of deacons, in the resolution of church conflicts and in the establishment of local church leadership (as in the Pauline churches), people who were schooled by the elders in the art of leadership followed that model.

Sometimes the eldership model worked very well; other times it needed supervision. In general, it worked well when the church did not encounter difficult, new challenges but needed only to maintain its equilibrium. In times of crisis, however (except for Acts 15), a different style of leadership was more helpful.

Today there continues to be a desire to return to the pristine models of the New Testament.[3] The question, "What is the New Testament model," comes up in relation to almost every issue confronting the modern church.

The answer must be, "There is no one New Testament model, unless it is that of experimentation." In biblical times there were truly many ways of doing things. If there is any model at all, it is that Jesus and the apostles were not bound by tradition. They developed new ways of solving the problems that were unique to their movement.

In this light, the desire of some contemporary church leaders to return to the eldership model of church government must be based on some foundation other than its being *the* New Testament model. For some churches the eldership model is right, but for others it may not be right. Every church has the obligation of searching out a model that is suitable for it and its particular mission in its own community. That is the true model of the New Testament.

A Custodial/Supervisory Leadership Style

In terms of providing general long-term care for churches, the apostle Paul was sensitive to needs, strong in caring for problems and flexible in adapting strategies to specific situations. His first concern was to establish churches, appoint elders and keep in touch with them. As problems arose he suggested adjustments, sometimes mandating corrective measures or sending in associates to deal with problems.

He did not feel that when a church was finally freestanding and independent it was able to care for all its needs. Neither, on the other hand, did he maintain tight control over it. He worked with the local leadership as closely as he could, always maintaining the healthy tension that must exist between leader and followers. Even after a decade or more he continued to offer counsel and guidance to his established churches, Corinth and Ephesus.

A review of these six leadership styles found in the Bible shows that certain styles are more appropriate than are other styles for certain types of situations. They also show that God is flexible and is able to use a variety of styles to accomplish his work.

This study should help free us from the notion that there is only one right biblical model, or even one right New Testament model. It should help us become more able to accept variations in leadership style, to adapt our styles to fit the situations we are in and to be flexible if the situation calls for flexibility.

Finally, we should be aware that this chapter has not given attention to the leadership styles of Jesus. A study of his leadership styles would bring another whole dimension to an evaluation of Christian leadership.

Perhaps Jesus' words in John 16:13 say it best. "When he, the Holy Spirit is come to you, he will guide you *into* all truth, for he will take what belongs to me and show it to you."

1. Willard Claassen, *Learning to Lead*, Scottdale, Penn.: Herald Press, 1963.

2. William Steuart McBirnie, *The Search for the Twelve Apostles*, Wheaton, Ill.: Tyndale House, 1973.

3. See Alexander Strauch, *Biblical Eldership: An Urgent Call to Restore Biblical Church Leadership*, 2nd ed., Littleton, Colo.: Lewis and Roth, 1988, with leader's guide, as one example of recent studies on this topic.

PART THREE

PSYCHOLOGY:
HOW PERSONALITY
DIFFERENCES
INFLUENCE CONFLICT

CHAPTER SEVEN

Personality Clashes and Forgiveness

Just as there are different styles of leadership, so also there are differences in personality. That was true in biblical times and it is also true today.

When I was younger I was influenced by the concept that a Christian should not experience personality clashes. In fact, to be repelled from a person because of a personality clash was a sin for me. Yet there were people who made me uncomfortable. In fact, just getting physically close to them was difficult. Talking to them was almost more than I could bear. I viewed that problem as "carnal" and truly felt guilty about it.

Much of that frustration has disappeared over the years. I still grieve that I cannot relate to everyone with equal ease. However, I now understand the natural human reasons why that is true. I also know more about the spiritual grace that is required to overcome it.

In this chapter we want to look at several ways to understand personality differences and what to do about them.

Personality Factors in Conflict

Type A / Type B Differences

In 1956 Dr. Meyer Friedman of the Harold Brunn Institute in San Francisco began researching the question whether certain personality traits affected heart disease. He also wanted to know if such traits had a bearing on a person's life span. His research spanned a period of more than twenty years. During that time he and his team verified beyond a doubt that certain types of behavior were always present in the lives of men below the age of sixty who had coronary disease. He also verified that those types of behavior affected other elements of their lives. These included social patterns, work habits and domestic relationships.

The same susceptibility to coronary disease was discovered to be true among women with similar behavior traits. These traits Dr. Friedman labeled the Type A behavior pattern. He called its opposite pattern Type B.[1]

What is important for us is that Type A behavior frequently causes tension and pain among the associates and co-workers of a Type A person. Friedman discovered that Type A leaders were frequently lonely, unfulfilled persons. They demanded more of themselves than was healthy for them and more often than not demanded the same of their colleagues and employees. These inappropriate demands often left persons feeling hurt, wounded, used and rejected, while the Type A person did not realize what had happened.

To the extent that Type A behavior causes tension and unrest among workers in the church and in Christian organizations, it bears serious scrutiny by the Lord's servants.

Friedman defined Type A behavior as "above all a continuous struggle, an unremitting attempt to accomplish or achieve more and more things or participate in more and more events in less and less time, frequently in the face of opposition . . . from other persons."[2]

It is often this type of opposition that causes some Christian leaders to perceive every policy (and polity) debate as a personal rejection of their authority. Rather than simply accepting differences of opinion as being Type A related (they may also be due to an honest difference in perspective), they see it as a sinister plot of the devil to defeat the cause of Christ as they understand it.

Characteristics of Type A behavior include one or more of the following: (1) domination by covert insecurity of status, or (2) hyperaggressiveness, or both, which cause the struggle to begin; (3) a sense of time urgency designated as hurry sickness; (4) easily aroused anger, termed free-floating hostility; and (5) a tendency toward self-destruction.[3]

For our purposes, it should be observed that some Christian leaders exhibit trait (1) whereas others exhibit trait (2). It may not always be clear which trait applies in any particular case. The observable symptoms and the outcome may be the same. Friedman makes the point that in either case the negative aspects of Type A traits can be treated successfully. It is possible for such persons to learn to lead normal, productive, happy, carefree lives.

As we have pointed out earlier and will again, energy levels are naturally higher in some people than in others. When such higher energy levels link up with Type A hyperaggressiveness the desire to dominate may become very strong. It may become so strong that an indifference to the feelings or rights of others can easily hinder effective Christian work. To the extent that such tendencies cause tension between people, they should surely be brought before the Lord for treatment and modification.[4]

The Myers-Briggs Type Indicator

In 1942 Isabel Myers and her mother, Katharine Briggs, put together their first personality type indicator. It was based on half a century of reflection, reading and study and was an effort to understand the positive aspects of some of the many differences in personality.

Their primary goal was finding a way to strengthen relationships between people. Over a period of three decades Myers tested 15,000 medical and nursing students and countless high school and college students in western Pennsylvania. Her goal was to develop a psychometrically sound instrument which could help people relate to each other better in spite of their personality differences.

Since 1975 the Myers-Briggs Type Indicator (MBTI) has been published by Consulting Psychologists Press (Palo Alto, Calif.) and evaluated by the research facilities of the Center for Applications of Psychological Type at the University of Florida in Gainesville. By 1990 it was the most widely used psychological test in the world for determining personality strengths in job development and in the enhancement of personal relationships. In that same year over two million copies of the test were administered in the United States and over one million copies were administered in Japan.

The flagship publication for the MBTI is *Gifts Differing* by Isabel Briggs Myers.[5] The dedication page states simply, "To all who desire to make better use of their gifts," and the following page quotes Romans 12:4-8. Another book, *Please Understand Me* by Keirsey and Bates, popularizes the application of the MBTI to marriage, career, parenting and leadership. It also provides a valuable three-page description of each of the sixteen possible types.[6]

The goal of the MBTI is not to measure what is "wrong" with an individual, but to help describe how persons really are and how they prefer to relate to others. In other words, it tells what is right about their personality styles. In theological terms, it is an effort to understand more fully how God created each person "in a fearful and wonderful way" (Ps. 139:14). That way each person can learn more fully how to realize his/her own potential and understand better how to relate to the persons around him/her.

The MBTI does not measure everything about the personality, but it does describe four primary traits that relate to decision-making and communication. It tells whether a person prefers to live privately (I=inside him/herself) or publicly (E=outwardly, with other persons around him/her); enjoys the realities of life (S) or prefers to contemplate the mystery and inventive potential of life (N); makes decisions by logic (T) or by what "feels" right (F); and prefers to organize his/her life (J) or just let it flow (P). When a person understands how s/he is different from others in these four areas, s/he can much more easily learn how to relate to others without always clashing.[7]

The MBTI, used with the Meier-Meisgeier Type Indicator for Children (MMTIC), makes it possible to help parents understand how to relate better to each other, to their teenage youth and to their children as early as the second grade. It helps parents know how to reduce stress in the home that is due to a lack of understanding in terms of each other's innate differences. It also helps them know how to help their children study and do their schoolwork better. In churches, it can be an invaluable tool for helping church staffs, councils, boards, committees and other groups come to understand each other (and their pastor) better. That is equally true for parachurch Christian organizations.

When we plot MBTI profiles on an organizational grid, it is possible to identify four different orientations to decision-making. These include: (1) let's keep it the way it is; (2) let's change it; (3) let's do it; or (4) let's evaluate it. When we know how each person in a group fits into the total picture it is easier to develop a better decision-making dynamic for groups in conflict. Thus the group can reduce stress and develop a better working relationship.[8]

Several implications for churches and groups in conflict emerge from a study of MBTI differences. One is the difference between flexibility and stability. S and J types tend to be more stable and therefore are able to accept change less easily (they see things as more "black and white" than others do). N and P types are more flexible in their attitudes and can accept change much more easily. Therefore they can adapt more easily to the demands for change around them.

If a group is aware of its overall MBTI profile it can use the S and J types to lend stability to the group. It can also learn to rely on the N and P types to help the group adapt to the changes in life around them. Such insights can help groups avoid the quarrelling which often occurs over which direction to take in program planning.

Another implication is that N types tend to have a broader range of vision in their perspective. S types tend to have a narrower range, but also have a sharper view of a single aspect of the issue. To put it another way, Ns can see the big picture but not all the details in it. Ss can see more of the details in a smaller portion of the picture. Again, if people do not understand those differences, they can expect a lot more quarrelling and frustration than otherwise.

Two other implications are that Es tend to talk more than Is, so with an E around one always knows what the score is. With an I around, one never quite knows the whole score, unless one asks. Also, Js need to have all the details nailed down tightly, while the Ps are much more comfortable letting nature take its course. Both types can complement each other, but they have to know how to do so to make it work.

One good rule of thumb for making organizations work better is to encourage the ISs to keep lifting up the values of the group; allow the Ns to dream the dreams; and be grateful for the ESs who are simply content to do the work.

The Four Temperaments

In 1966 Tim LaHaye first published his best-selling book, *Spirit-Controlled Temperament*. He followed that with *Understanding the Male Temperament* and more recently with *I Love You, But Why Are We So Different*.[9]

LaHaye based his approach to understanding personality on the early Greek medical model of attributing physical reactions to the four fluids of the body. These are blood, water, black bile and yellow bile. We now know that the four body fluids do not directly control our behavior. Still, the four temperament type descriptions do give us another way of understanding differences between people.

The Sanguine (blood) person is warm, lively and full of life. S/he is open to life and other people, extroverted, bouncy and positively oriented. S/he can easily become the life of the party, even if s/he does not know a soul in the room at the outset.

The Choleric (water) is hot-tempered, active, quick to react, practical and strong-willed. S/he is always sure of her/himself, not frightened by obstacles and can easily become a workaholic. S/he is a crusader, an achiever and strongly committed to the projects and tasks s/he undertakes.

The Melancholic (black bile) is a perfectionist, analytical, self-sacrificing, gifted and very sensitive emotionally. S/he is generally introverted, faithful and dependable. S/he is able to diagnose problems when s/he encounters them and find solutions for them.

The Phlegmatic (yellow bile) is calm, cool, collected and easy-going. S/he is well-balanced with a low boiling point. Pressures do not phase him/her; s/he is more interested in enjoying people and events in life. His/her rare sense of humor is highly entertaining for the more serious types of people.

LaHaye has developed a word association test by which he is able to help interested persons find their type, their secondary types and their opposite or negative traits. His books are replete with ideas and suggestions for strengthening one's gifts and refining one's weaknesses. A committed Christian, he writes with ample biblical examples and uses Christian principles freely. He includes a coupon in his books by which a person can secure copies of the temperament test.

The Personal Profile System (DISC)

Many years ago psychologist William Marston developed a fourfold trait-based description of behavioral styles which seemed to describe most individuals. The work was further refined by John Geier and Dorothy Downey in the 1970s and adapted for the workplace. Ken Voges and Ron Braund added biblical correlations to help Christians better understand their behaviors from a biblical perspective. This approach provides a tool for Christian leaders for guiding individuals to realize more fully their potential without being hurtful to others in the process of developing their leadership style.[10]

The Personal Profile System helps an individual understand how s/he prefers to respond to various influences and organizational elements of life. It can also help families, boards, committees and work groups gain a clearer picture of how each of them responds differently to tasks and relationships. Consequently, each person can learn to make adjustments which makes life go more smoothly.

One of the four identified styles is Dominance. These individuals prefer to be in control of their environment. They take charge of events and shape their environment by overcoming opposition. They desire to see results and can easily run over others in the attempt.

Another style is Influencing. These individuals are relationally oriented and work at bringing people into alliances which accomplish group goals. They are less task-oriented and may allow technical details to slip by for the sake of protecting individual comfort zones.

The Steadiness style prefers to cooperate with others in accomplishing goals. They prefer teamwork over working alone and do not mind performing routine, repetitive tasks. The joy comes in doing things together, more than in accomplishing the goal.

Compliance is identified as the style that desires quality control. They appreciate structure and order and prefer working with groups that emphasize quality in products and services. They tend to be logical and perfectionist in their approach to life.

In addition to identifying the dominant style of the individual, the Personal Profile System identifies and correlates the secondary trait. In so doing a total of fifteen classic styles are available for study. In combination with a study of the personality profiles of biblical persons, it provides extremely helpful insights into God's creative work within each of us.

Emotional Pain

Whatever personality inventory we consult in an attempt to understand ourselves and others better, one very important personality factor is always left out. That is the impact of emotional trauma and pain upon otherwise well-rounded personality descriptions.

Emotional pain can come from a variety of sources. These may include deep disappointments in life, traumatic loss of friends and family members, a variety of abuses and a host of obsessions. Many of these scarring elements of life are now part of the new term "personality deficiency syndrome."

One element of the new studies emerging out of an awareness of emotional pain is the impact that painful childhood experiences have on our adult lives. The decade of the eighties gave us the term *Adult Children of Alcoholics,* or ACOAs. Broadly speaking, the term includes persons "who came from homes where a parent was addicted to alcohol, drugs, work, gambling, or refers to one whose parent abused or grossly neglected them."

The term can also include homes where parents are too strict and controlling, including rigid religious homes. Charles Sell, from whose book the above quotation comes, was one of the first to write about ACOAs and their journey to emotional healing from the standpoint of a committed Christian.[11]

The terms "dysfunctional families" and "codependency" have also been coined as a result of similar studies. The literature is still emerging and has not been fully applied yet to organizational conflict. However, several significant books are already available.[12]

The importance of this discussion for resolving conflicts in Christian groups is that: (1) Conflict is not necessarily due to sin. (2) Conflict may be due to differences between people which they do not fully understand. (3) Conflict may also be due to the effects of emotional scarring that does not allow the individual to develop fully into a healthy adult Christian. Any emotional scarring can cloud an otherwise positive personality trait or magnify an otherwise benign personality weakness.

If we do not deal with our emotional pain in a responsible manner, no amount of revival or spiritual exercise will provide a full remedy for our conflicts. No amount of confession, forgiveness, or prayer will effectively bring lasting peace.

It is precisely here that the apostle Paul's prayer for psychological wholeness in 1 Thessalonians 5:23 is most appropriate and most needed. It is for this reason that churches and Christian groups must find ways to include counseling and effective emotional therapy in their repertoire of ministries in today's world.

Issues of Power

The discussion above, brief though it was, had to precede the forthcoming issues. There is no other way to deal compassionately, intelligently, or realistically with issues of power unless one first understands the psychology of personality and emotional pain.

If we remember that power has to do with the ability to get things done,[13] we also must be aware that power comes to people in several different ways. In this section we will discuss some of them briefly.

Pecking Order

The "pecking order" describes the way in which people in groups arrange themselves when it comes to determining whose word has the most weight.

Several factors may determine who has more relative power in a group. The least important of them is official rank or election to office. Factors such as prestige, practical knowledge, ability to relate to others, permission of the group to act as an influencer and force of personality are much more important.

Having a high rank in the pecking order in one group does not necessarily mean that an individual will have a high rank in every group. Rank in the pecking order is always relative, closely connected to the relationship of others in the group and the depth of concern an individual has about issues in that group. The rank may even vary within the group, depending upon which issue the group is concerned about at any given time.

Whenever someone leaves the group there is often an unconscious scramble to see who can move up in rank. Other times there is a similar scramble when issues change or personal comfort zones are challenged.

A particularly important scramble occurs when there is a change in pastoral (or chief executive officer or other supervisor) leadership. The incoming leader almost invariably occupies a different position in the pecking order from the predecessor and is attracted to different people in the organization or group. This rearrangement of the pecking order can often cause unexpected intense jealousies and bitter rivalries.

A wise leader (board/committee chairperson, CEO, supervisor, or pastor) will strive to occupy a position somewhere between the very top and the very middle of the spectrum. If the leader occupies a spot too low on the spectrum, s/he will be overpowered by those above him/her. If the leader is too close to the very top in real power, s/he will lose touch with those at the low end of the spectrum.

Energy Levels and Flow

Some people are highly motivated and strongly energized, while others seem to creep along slowly. When persons of opposite energy levels are expected to work closely together they will always experience some discomfort. To work together harmoniously they must adjust their output levels so they can work more closely together at the same speed. It is not true that one is lazy and the other is out of control. God made people very differently and energy levels and flow is one of those differences.

Energy flow relates to how energy moves. In some people, it moves in strong (or not so strong) spurts of energy, while in others it moves in a steady stream. The difference is similar to the difference between AC and DC electrical current. For some, it flows best when they are with people, while for others it flows best when they are working alone. Some can function better when there is noise around them and others can do good work only when it is quiet.

Such differences as these can often create the illusion of a personality clash. If it is possible to identify exactly what it is that is causing the clash, it is fairly easy to make adjustments. Such adjustments can then reduce the uneasiness enough so that people can survive together more compatibly. Their own personal energy level and flow can then be more fully expressed in another context.

Circles of Influence

Another issue of power is the circle of influence within which a person moves. Very few people live totally isolated from other human beings. We are usually affected by the views, feelings and concerns of others.

No one is able to relate equally to everyone else in a group. Although cliques are almost universally despised, they are essential for our emotional survival. They provide a manageable zone of comfort within which we are able to move about freely.

Circles of influence are made up of concentric spheres, the innermost of which is composed of one's closest friends. Around that sphere are the persons whom we know quite well and upon whom we depend to help us get things done in life. A third sphere is composed of acquaintances who fill out the corners of our life and in many ways enrich our lives.

Circles of influence may vary for any individual, depending upon what is happening in his/her life at the time. There may be one circle of influence in the neighborhood where s/he lives, another where s/he works and a third at church or in another significant group setting.

An individual's placement within the circles of power of any group also may vary. Any individual may be in the center circle of influence at work, in a secondary circle of power at church and out on the fringes in the extended family.

The amount of energy that a person exerts in any given circumstance may depend upon several factors. These include how significantly the situation affects the person, his/her significant others and the goals in life. It may also depend upon physical energy levels, the amount of time s/he has to commit, the amount of support or encouragement from people in his/her own circles of influence and the amount of cooperation s/he receives from friends.

If lots of energy and commitment are forthcoming from any given circle of influence, that circle of people may rise far above what might otherwise be expected of them. That is also true if their affectual needs or goals rank high on their priority list. Adversely, if the group of people cannot commit extensively due to any combination of factors, they may appear to default in their commitment to a given cause.

In understanding and dealing with the conflicts between persons and groups of persons, all aspects of the relationship between differing circles of influence must be taken keenly into account.

Keepers of the Gate

Keepers of the gate have been defined in literature on group dynamics as those persons who allow new individuals to enter the group. They are also the ones who allow group members to modify the traditions and customs of the group. The degree to which they contribute to issues of conflict depends upon their placement in the circles of influence of the group. It also depends upon their conflict management styles and their sensitivity to the needs of everyone in the group.

Keepers of the gate may be almost anyone in the group. They may be easily identified or they may be hard to detect. They may be the elected leaders of the group, or more likely the unsung pillars of stability in the group. They may be vocal strong persons or they may be the quiet ones, beloved by all, whom no one would dare to offend. It is essential to take these important persons of the group into account. Otherwise individuals will almost surely fail in their efforts to resolve successfully many church or organizational group conflicts.

In chapter three Oliver functioned as a "keeper of the gate" in Elm Street Church. As long as people took seriously his complaints about light bulbs , conflict and controversy continued to flourish. They could have conducted an efficiency survey on the physical plant. In this way they could have determined the degree to which burning light bulbs contributed to the financial plight of the church. Oliver probably would have been embarrassed, but the conflict could have been ended conclusively. It was easier to ignore the problem because of their esteem for Oliver.

Churches and organizations grow in the same way that trees grow—by one growth ring per year. The farther away from the center new people become, the less access to real power they have. If the center rings are composed of "hard wood" as opposed to "soft wood," penetration is virtually impossible.

Churches and organizations become integrated in approximately the same way one makes marble cake. I used to watch my mother pour a layer of white cake mix into the pan, then a chocolate layer, then another white layer and then another chocolate layer. Then she would take a knife and weave it back and forth in the pan until the layers were thoroughly intermixed. After baking, the cake presented beautiful contours of white and chocolate waves.

If someone does not take the responsibility for intermixing new people and long-time members or planning for its occurrence, it will likely never happen. Layer after layer of small interest groups will develop without becoming an integral part of the fabric of the group or church. Without adequate integration, power struggles and lack of appreciation for each other's views will always be a part of the group and negative conflict will never cease.

Strategies for Change

Conflicts require change. When different goals and desires come into contact they clash. That clashing requires change.

We can change by default, because one is stronger or louder or more powerful than the other. However, it is better to change because we choose to use a strategy that works in a fair manner. We can all seek to be winners by applying the divine wisdom that God gives us to overcome all obstacles. There are a few important strategies for change.

Permission Giving

God is the greatest permission giver of all time. He does not always like to do so, but he chooses to because he created us with the freedom of choice.

God chose to let Adam and Eve disobey him in the Garden of Eden and then he chose to go to them seeking reconciliation.

God chose to let Moses strike the rock instead of speaking to it twice. He also chose to punish him by keeping him out of the land of promise.

Jesus Christ chose to include talkative Peter, tempestuous James and John and scheming Judas in his trusted band of twelve disciples. He also chose to endure many of their weaknesses in order to prepare them adequately for service.

Permission giving recognizes that people are the way they are through divine creation as well as through human frailty. It seeks to work with them as well as possible, given who they are. Permission giving recognizes that people are different. It does not seek to change them in an artificial manner. It allows us to fulfill all the capabilities within ourselves and allows others to fulfill all the capabilities within themselves. Permission giving presents options and allows others to make choices on their own volition.

Six principles of Christian permission giving, which allow people to be more fully themselves, may be summarized in this way:

1. Give life permission to be just the way it is. You cannot change it anyway!
2. Be who you are — responsibly.
3. Let others be who they are — caringly.
4. Be willing to say "where" you are — kindly.
5. Let others say "where" they are — acceptingly.
6. Care about your sister or brother — appropriately.

Reframing the Interests

Reframing the interests means looking at the problem in a different way.

We can perhaps all recall the fable of the six blind men who went to the forest to learn about an elephant.[14] One got hold of the elephant's tail and said, "The elephant is like a rope." Another got hold of his flapping ear and said, "The elephant is like a fan." A third felt the elephant's leg and said, "The elephant is like a tree." A fourth felt his side and said, "The elephant is like a wall." A fifth took hold of the trunk and said, "The elephant is like a snake." The sixth felt the elephant's tusk and said, "The elephant is like a spear." Obviously they were all wrong and yet at the same time all of them were right. The differences between them came only as a result of their limited perspectives.

As humans, we are all limited in our ability to see things clearly. Oliver, of Elm Street Church, did not intend to keep his beloved church tied up in conflict and controversy; he only wanted to save money. He did not realize how incomplete his vision was in relation to the whole issue of finance.

Reframing the interests (defining the problem differently) in the case of Elm Street Church could have meant talking about different ways to save money. A little research might have revealed that many more dollars could be saved by repairing the weather stripping around the windows and doors. Elm Street Church could have defined the "interests" more broadly as "saving money," instead of "turning out lights to save money." In this way they could have been much more constructive in their efforts.

Just as in the description of the elephant, people in conflict can learn to say, "My view of the issue is . . ." and "My view of the issue is . . ." etc., until each person's viewpoint is on the table. Then the next question to ask would be, "What do you really want to get out of this discussion? What is your goal?"

The blind men would have said, "We all want to know what an elephant is like." Oliver would have said, "I want to save money." With the basic underlying issue out in the open, alternative (and sometimes composite) ways of accomplishing that goal can be developed. Such alternate approaches would satisfy more people and reduce the conflict immensely.

That is exactly what Solomon did in 1 Kings 3:16-27. Each woman's goal was to have the baby. Solomon changed the goal to one of life for the baby. Suddenly having the baby was not as important as keeping the baby alive. The real mother quickly came forward and presumably both women agreed to share the responsibility of raising the child. The king preserved both justice and personal integrity and the women learned to problem solve on a higher plane.

Forgiveness

Forgiveness is also a biblical concept, as we all know. James teaches us to "confess your faults one to another and pray for one another, that you may be healed" (5:16). There is a spiritual dimension to this aspect of healing in the Christian life, just as there is a physical dimension.

Ron Claassen of Mennonite Conciliation Service—West Coast[15] points out that forgiveness is a two-way reconciliation process. It involves confession, a restoration of equity and a pledge to let the future be better.

In the first step both sides must admit to each other what occurred between them to damage the relationship. The one who did wrong must admit the wrong actions and the wrong attitudes. The other must admit the fears/anger/jealousy, etc. that were experienced when the misdeed occurred.

In the second step both sides must agree on what it will take to restore balance between them. It may include restitution, apology, better listening skills, clearer communication, more permission for each to be themselves, or greater effort at equalizing the balance of power between them.

In the third step Claassen advocates writing up and signing a covenant that states explicitly in what specific ways each side will respond to the other. The written covenant is important, because if the individuals only make the agreement verbally, they must work harder and show greater trust and collaboration in keeping the agreement in force. That is often hard when a relationship is already seriously damaged.

Assertive Caring Assistance

Just because people may be willing to forgive each other does not guarantee that they will not sin against each other again in the same way. Old patterns die hard. New patterns require time to develop.

Sometimes parties who once experienced alienation require individual and group coaching to learn how to develop new patterns of communication and behavior. They can get this help from a caring person within the organization or from a professional outside it.

A caring pastor, executive officer or lay leader faced with the responsibility of guiding people in the midst of conflict must have a strong sense of what is right for the whole group. S/he also must have a healthy enough sense of personal self-esteem so as not to be threatened by other weaker individuals who use their emotions poorly.

S/he must use positive, assertive talk to show the difference between acceptable and unacceptable behavior. Hints and mere suggestions are not enough. Talk must be direct, clear, plain and simple.

It is best if such talk is in the second person, active voice. "When she fails to show respect to you, you must kindly but firmly remind her that showing respect is part of her job expectation." That is far better than saying, "You might suggest to her that courtesy is a Christian virtue and say that it would be good if there could be more respect shown by office personnel."

The five rules of assertive talk for helping others develop better relational and behavioral habits are:[16]

1. Maintain firm boundaries. Be clear about what is acceptable and what is not.

2. Present positive options. Do not only say what is wrong. Also say what is acceptable and offer more than one possibility so the other person can participate in selecting his/her own appropriate behaviors.

3. Provide loving, caring support. There will always be some emotional confusion in reconstructing attitudes and behavior. Stay with the person long enough to help him/her work through those points of confusion and let the feelings finish.

4. Ask for full compliance. Do not allow half-choices. If you expect respect, expect complete respect. If deadlines are to be honored, expect them to be fully honored. Be clear and firm in working toward that goal, but allow for time to develop better and more focused habits.

5. Use supervisory persons/committees to maintain integrity. Move one level up in the organization to select a supervisor who can help the individual/s maintain their new commitments. Hold the supervisor accountable to you for the success of the project.

1. Meyer Friedman and Diane Ulmer, *Treating Type A Behavior — and Your Heart*, New York: Alfred A. Knopf, 1984. Type B men are those who have none of the five characteristics of the Type A personality, pp.71-80. Type B persons were found to be just as active in leadership as Type A persons. In one recent study 62% of top male leaders were Type A and 39% were Type B, in a population where 75% of all males were Type A, pp.81-82.

2. Friedman and Ulmer, p.31.

3. Friedman and Ulmer, p.31. Three components generate Type A behavior in men: lack of adequate unconditional love by the mother in infancy and childhood, appropriate levels of affection and encouragement in personal growth and development from one or both of his parents (p.45). In addition to unconditional love from his mother, the Type A man seems to need a mother pleasant enough in appearance and sufficiently intelligent and educated for the child to be proud of (p.48). Type A behavior in women develops when the similar lack of a positive relationship exists between the woman and her father. The lack of two-way communication was found to be an important missing ingredient in the lives of both men and women (p.85). [Author's note: Type A behavior may also be a learned behavior trait passed down from a Type A parent. Moreover it may be manifested differently in outgoing persons than in quieter types of persons.]

4. Friedman and Ulmer, p.33. In a recent four-year study it was demonstrated beyond doubt that Type A behavior is directly responsible for coronary heart disease. Counseling and behavior modification significantly decreased the risks up to 30% in that study alone. See p.142.

5. Isabel Briggs Myers, *Gifts Differing*, Palo Alto, Calif.: Consulting Psychologists Press, 1980.

6. David Keirsey and Marilyn Bates, *Please Understand Me:*

Character and Temperament Types, Costa Mesa, Calif.:Matrix Books, 1978.

7. Current type distributions based on 250,000 samples as reported in McCaulley, Macdaid and Kainz, "Estimated Frequencies of the MBTI Types," *Journal of Psychological Type* IX (1985):3-9, indicate that there are more Es than Is overall; more Es in women than in men; more Ss than Ns overall; F in females = ca. 66%; T in males = ca. 65% to 70%; Js are 60% to 65%; Ps are 35% to 40%; dependable ISJs = ca. one-third of the tested population; STJ is more frequent among men, SFJ more frequent among women; INs are relatively infrequent, but more oriented toward academic pursuits. (Thus, seminary-educated pastors likely tend to be INs, whereas conservative church members tend to be SJs. Liberal church members may be expected to have more NPs.)

8. For more information on using the MBTI in churches and organizations, see the order form at the back of this book (Appendix B), or contact the author at Resources for Resolving Life's Issues, Colorado Springs, Colorado, 1-800-477-3007.

9. Tim LaHaye, *Spirit-Controlled Temperament*, Wheaton, Ill.: Tyndale House, 1966; *Understanding Male Temperament: What Every Man Would Like to Tell His Wife About Himself...But Won't*, Old Tappan, N.J.: Fleming H. Revell, 1977; *I Love You, But Why Are We So Different: Making the Differences Work for You*, Eugene Ore.: Harvest House, 1991; see also Florence Littauer, *Personality Plus: How to Understand Others By Understanding Yourself*, Tarrytown, N.Y.:Fleming H. Revell, 1983.

10. William M.Marston, *Emotions of Normal People*, New York: Harcourt Brace, 1928; Ken Voges and Ron Braund, *Understanding How Others Misunderstand You*, Chicago: Moody Press, 1990. A self-guiding workbook is also available.

11. Charles Sell, *Unfinished Business: Helping Adult Children Resolve Their Past*, Portland, Ore.: Multnomah Press, 1989, p. 9.

12. See e.g., Cruse and Cruse, *Understanding Co-dependency*, Deerfield Beach, Fla.: Health Communications, 1990; Henfelt,

Minirth and Meier, *Love is a Choice: Recovery for Codependent Relationships*, Nashville, Tenn.: Thomas Nelson, 1989; Pat Springle, *Rapha's 12-Step Program for Overcoming Codependency*, Houston, Tex.: Rapha Publishing/Word, 1990; David Mains, *Healing the Dysfunctional Church Family*, Wheaton, Ill.: Victor Books, 1992; James Qualben, *Peace in the Parish*, San Antonio, Tex.: Langmarc, 1991, chap.10.

13. See the last section of chapter four. See also Roy Oswald, *Power Analysis of a Congregation*, Washington, D.C.: Alban Institute, 1980.

14. "Six Blind Men and an Elephant," an old East Indian folk tale elaborated on in James Riordan, *An Illustrated Treasury of Fairy and Folk Tales*, Twickenham: Hamlyn, 1986.

15. Ron Claassen, Center for Conflict Studies and Peacemaking, Fresno Pacific College, 1717-So. Chestnut, Fresno, Calif. 93072.

16. See also Ruth Koch and Kenneth Haugk, *Speaking the Truth in Love: How to be an Assertive Christian*, St. Louis: Stephen Ministries, 1992.

CHAPTER EIGHT

Managing Your Emotions in a Conflict

O LORD, you have searched me and you know me. . . . You created my inmost being; you knit me together in my mother's womb. I praise you because I am fearfully and wonderfully made; your works are wonderful, I know that full well (Ps. 139:1,13-14).

May God himself, the God of peace, sanctify you through and through. May your whole spirit, soul and body be kept blameless at the coming of our Lord Jesus Christ (1 Thess. 5:23).

The bottom line in all conflict is individual discomfort. When an individual reaches the end of his/her tolerance zone nothing in the world will stop a defensive action or reaction from occurring. All the theology and all the biblical teaching in the world will not prevail under such circumstances. For this reason, it is essential to know something about how emotions work. Without that knowledge all the rules of conflict management will ultimately leave us shortchanged.

There are two advantages in coming to understand our own emotions and the emotions of others. First, we will be able to negotiate differences better without taking things as personally as we otherwise might. Second, we will not get upset so quickly at others.

For many years already I have thought that all feelings could be divided into the two major categories of positive feelings and negative feelings. More recently I have revised the categories into feelings which bring pleasure and feelings which are designed to protect us from harm.

The only successful method I know for avoiding bad emotional consequences in our relationships is to know how each type of feeling or emotion works and what its early warning signs are. That way we may put Ephesians 4:26 into practice so we do not sin when we experience a "protective" emotion.

How Feelings Work

The Bible gives us clear teaching on the matter of dealing with emotions. We need not fear our feelings, for they are created by God (Ps. 139:13) who gave them to us both to enhance our lives and to protect us from danger.

Paul prays in 1 Thessalonians 5:23 that our spirit (*pneuma*), soul (*pseuche*) and body (*soma*) may be preserved blameless until Christ comes. Christian teaching provides clear answers for the care of the spirit and the body. Clear teaching for the care of the soul, however (*pseuche* includes our feelings and emotions), has been slow in coming.

A good Christian approach to psychology is finally becoming well developed. It is no longer necessary to fear that all psychology is humanistic and ungodly. Second Corinthians 10:5 encourages us to "take captive every thought to make it obedient to Christ." As psychologists who are thoroughly Christian continue to practice and teach and write, we may become more and more confident that we will discover God's answers to the healing of the emotions.

Stanley Keleman, a medical researcher, writes that

> ...emotional anatomy is layers of skin and muscle, more muscles, organs, more organs, bone and the invisible layer of hormones as well as the organization of experience... Anatomical relationship is also emotional relationship. Pulsating organs generate good feeling, a sense of well-being, pleasure. Constricted, spastic, bloated or weak tissue gives rise to pain, discomfort, unpleasant feelings about one's self. Anatomy and feeling are also behavioral relationships. Any breakdown in anatomical or emotional organization results in an equivalent breakdown in behavior.

In other words, our emotions are produced by the tension or relaxation of skin, muscles and organs, the secretion of hormones and the illness or health of the various parts of our body. Those feelings or emotions, whether pleasant or protective, cause us to act and react in certain ways as we attend to the needs of our bodies and spirits.

That is why neither theology nor Bible verses can stem the tide of strong feelings. Only training and commitment to deeply held, firmly entrenched principles can guard us and guide us in the most extreme emotional situations of life.

Six Basic Emotions

We all recognize that there are many individual emotions. However, most of those feelings can be grouped around six basic emotions, according to Dixie and Frank Morris.[2] All other emotions are complex configurations of those basic six.

The six basic emotions are visually represented in the diagram below. In some ways each pair functions as an opposite of the other, although that correlation must not be pushed too far. Nevertheless, in the reactions which each pair calls forth, they do relate to each other in rather important ways.

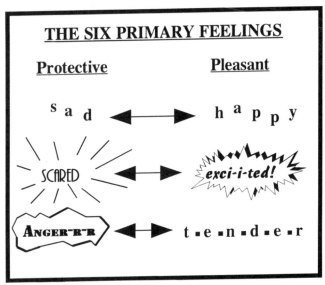

Happiness is the sensation of fulfillment. When happiness is sustained it turns into joy. Its biblical equivalent is *shalom*, a concept which speaks of everything in life being just right. There are no losses, no fears and no insults or attacks. Things are just the way we want them to be.

But there is one important catch. Happiness is always defined by our own individual standards. It is our own comfort zone that is at peace. The same set of circumstances that bring us satisfaction may leave another person very uncomfortable and unhappy.

Sadness is properly defined as the emotion of loss. When things which make us content disappear or do not even materialize, our lives become empty. When that happens, we cry because the structures of our body contract to fill the (emotional) void. As we cry that inner tension is relieved and crying soon stops.

Children cry easily because they have not yet learned to stifle their emotions. Adults refuse to allow their emotions full expression, because it hampers their work and makes them appear to be inefficient and unable to deal with life.

Excitement is the emotion of positive action. Any event or activity which we perceive as good for us calls for the excretion of huge amounts of adrenaline. That produces high levels of energy, which we can use to accomplish the activity or event with which we are absorbed.

Successful achievement of the goal leaves us feeling satisfied and successful. We say that it was a good experience; we had a good time. People who get very excited about a new project or task (or office in the church or other organization) often cannot slow down to adjust to the needs of others until their enthusiasm subsides.

Scare or startle is the emotion of protection from events or activities which may hurt us. It causes us to pull back, flee, fight, react verbally, or engage in other activities designed to protect us from harm.

In this case also huge amounts of adrenaline are secreted into the body system. This gives us extra energy and strength to provide for our own physical and emotional protection. When that happens we usually will not stop until we perceive that the danger is passed and we are safe again.

Tenderness is the sensation of closeness and togetherness in a trusting environment. It gives us the feeling that there is no threat of loss or fear of danger. We feel free to allow our emotions a full and free range of expression, expecting to be fully accepted and understood.

Sustained tenderness always turns into emotional love. It is deepened without fear until our own comfort zone or the comfort zone of the other is stretched to its limit. Then, as it seeks to move even further into the recesses of the heart, it is offended as we or the other suddenly draw back, fearing too much intimacy or self-exposure.

Anger is the emotion of offense. It occurs when another assaults our integrity, our reputation, or our abilities. It also can occur when another moves in too close to our personal tender spot, pulls back too soon, or does not continue to honor our openness to them. Such hurts create a jerkiness of our body tissues, often resulting in tears as we attempt to balance ourselves internally again.

The resulting reaction may include insults or assaults as we attempt to punish the offender. It may also result in flight as we seek to get as far away from the offender as possible. While openness and tenderness is the deepest and most intense of all emotions, anger is the most volatile. Herein undoubtedly lies the reason for the many biblical words concerning this most destructive of all emotions.

Emotions in the Bible

It is now time to look at what the Bible says about the three primary protective emotions. They are the ones which most often get us caught up in negative, destructive conflict with others.

Sadness is described in the Bible in terms which portray pain. The Hebrew term implies having an undesirable or disfigured face due to pain and the Greek term, *lupeó*, also portrays the pain of a loss. A good Old Testament example is Nehemiah's sadness (fallen countenance) after he had heard that the walls and gates of Jerusalem were still in ruin (Neh. 2:1-3).

One New Testament example is the experience of the young ruler who departed from Jesus with great sadness because he did not want to sell his possessions (Matt. 19:22). Another is the feelings of the disciples when Jesus told them about his coming betrayal (Matt. 26:22). The biblical solution for sadness is joy and gladness (Isa. 61:3).

Scare is usually described in the Bible by its more complex emotion, fear, although the Greek root, *phebomai*, has the connotation of startle. Fearing or being afraid is a sustained emotion due to the enduring presence of danger.

Adam feared God as long as his sin was not forgiven (Gen. 3:10) and Abram was afraid in a new land until after God had reassured him that everything was under control (Gen. 15:1). Israel feared the Egyptians until the Lord moved the pillar of cloud to protect them (Exod. 14:13) and Saul continually feared David because the threat of being overthrown never left him (1 Sam. 18:29).

Nebuchadnezzar was terrified by his dream (Dan. 4:5) and the sailors with whom Jonah sailed feared destruction in the storm (Jonah 1:5). Zechariah, Mary, the shepherds and the women feared the angel (Luke 1-2; Mark 16:8). Joseph feared public scorn (Matt. 1:20) and the revenge of Archelaus, Herod's son (Matt. 2:22). The disciples feared the storm (Mark 4:40) and also feared Jesus' rebuke at their question (Mark 9:32). The Jewish rulers feared the people when they wanted to arrest Jesus (Matt. 21:46).

The biblical solution for scare and fear is trust in God and his power. God will fight our enemies for us (Deut. 3:22) and care for us in times of uncertainty (Ps. 56:3; 118:6). God will sustain us so the shame and disgrace of the past will not overwhelm us (Isa. 54:4) and he will be our light and stronghold so no one can overpower us (Ps. 27:1).

Anger is spoken of many more times in the Bible than any other emotion. The words anger, angry and rage occur 259 times in the King James Version and 354 times in the New International Version. The two main Hebrew words indicate a snorting of the nostrils and a vexation of spirit. The main Greek term is *orgé*, suggesting an impulsive mental bent towards indignation.

Cain was angry because God did not appreciate his offering (Gen. 4:5) and Moses became enraged (his anger burned within him) when he saw the golden calf (Exod. 32:19). Sanballot and company were angered when the walls of Jerusalem were repaired (Neh. 4:7) and King Ahasuerus became furious when Queen Vashti did not present herself at his command (Esther 1:12).

Jesus expressed anger at the misuse of the temple, driving out those who profaned it by their merchandising (John 2:15; Matt. 21:12). Jacob recognized the danger of anger when he blessed his sons before his death, noting that often the result of anger was the action of killing and maiming (Gen. 49:6).

God also expressed anger, most often against the wickedness of humanity. Sometimes it resulted in death (Exod. 22:24) and punishment (Lev. 26:28). God was angry with Job's friends for their misspeaking (Job 42:7) and with Solomon for turning his heart away from the Lord (1 Kings 11:9). Because of Israel's sin the people lost their inheritance; the Lord's anger did not subside until he had fully accomplished his purpose in punishing Israel (Ps. 78:56-59, Jer. 17:4; 23:20, Ezek. 23:25).

God's anger, however, is not unpredictable or impulsive. He is "slow to anger, abounding in love and forgiving sin and rebellion" (Num. 14:18). "His anger lasts only a moment" (Ps. 30:5) and in his mercy he forgives iniquities (Ps. 78:38). He does not "always accuse, nor [does] he harbor his anger forever" (Ps. 103:9). He delights in showing mercy (Micah 7:18).

The biblical solution for anger is to confront it honestly, but also to manage it (Prov. 29:11) and not allow its rage to lead us into sinful actions (Ps. 4:4, Eph. 4:26). It is possible to bring it under control (Ps. 85:3, Col. 3:8, James 1:19). When confronting another person's anger, a gentle response keeps the conflict from escalating any more than necessary (Prov. 15:1).

Given this background, it is easy to see why Jesus would say that by God's standards anger towards another will be judged (evaluated to determine its validity). If that anger causes an individual to act or speak badly toward the other, the result will be punishment (Matt. 5:22-23).

Four Early Warning Signs

We learned in chapters two and seven that when our comfort zone and/or our personality style gets pushed too far, we tend to react defensively. This always produces conflict of some type and it is often destructive in nature.

One of the most important things we can do when conflict begins is to pay attention to the early warning signs of the protective emotions. They are present in all three cases (sadness, scare and anger), but they escalate more rapidly in each successive wave of emotion, becoming more intense and tending to last longer.

There are always four physical "early warning signs" as the body prepares for the danger it perceives to be present. Some are more intense and manifest themselves in different kinds of ways. While they function to prepare the body to protect itself, they are also helpful in alerting us to the danger of potential sin. Thus we can beware that we do not act out our feelings inappropriately.

The early warning signs are an accelerated heartbeat, rapid breathing, muscle tension (in preparation for physically defensive actions) and the escalation of energy produced by the secretion of adrenaline.

As all four of these physical functions combine to fend off the perceived danger, the body feels flushed and invigorated. Fists can fly, words can tumble out of the mouth and feet and legs can go into instant action. It is important, therefore, that we are prepared to direct our energies into the right paths so that sinful actions do not cause additional offenses.

114

It is one thing to note the early warning signs within us; it is quite another to be alert enough to notice them in others. It is possible, however. We can notice when another person is breathing rapidly, looks flushed, becomes nervous and fidgety, or manifests other physical signs of agitation. When that happens it is time to act appropriately to relieve the tension. It is extremely important at such times to offer a gentle answer and abate wrathful words (Prov. 15:1).

No new emotion will last longer than eight minutes.[3] Some emotions last only a minute or two. That is not hard to understand, for once the four physical functions are engaged, they cannot stop abruptly on command until they are finished.

As we become aware of that, we can be more patient and understanding of others when they become agitated. We can also be more in control of ourselves. We can feel sure that it will not be long until the other person has calmed down again and life will go on in normal fashion.

We can have the same assurance about ourselves.

Comfort Zones

Another element of emotion is that everyone is most comfortable in their own emotional environment. Persons who grew up in a hostile environment learned either to implode (keep their feelings to themselves) or explode violently (definitely let others know how they feel). Such a person does not relate well to threatening environments.

One who normally implodes emotions will probably walk away from even low levels of stress and tension. One who normally explodes will quickly intimidate others, but will only relate in a normal manner if others are equally explosive in their reply.

A person who grew up in a nurturing, caring environment may greatly fear a hostile person, for s/he did not learn to function well in the face of intense explosions. Thus the explosive person may interpret quietness as timidity or as accommodation, while the gentler person may interpret explosiveness as hostility when it is not meant that way at all.

Consequently, when individuals are faced with bridging the gap between hostile and timid persons in an organizational conflict, they must give attention to at least two separate issues. One is the way in which different emotional environments cause persons to speak past each other. The other is the levels of energy which each is willing to expend in order to actually relate to the other.

The explosive one will have to learn to soften his/her tones and the quiet one will have to learn to be more forceful. Such discipline will be hard for both, but it is essential to balance the communication relationship.

It is also important to let feelings happen (under your supervision) and finish, so they do not come back to hurt you again later. Any new emotion will escalate quickly and then, as we stated earlier, take from three to eight minutes to finish. That is because the heightened pulse rate, breathing rate, new levels of adrenaline and increased muscle tension cannot subside in a moment.

If you try to quench those physical reactions, the frustration of that quenching will be stored up in your emotional memory bank. Unfortunately, they will return one day for finishing in surprising and uncomfortable ways.

It is possible to supervise the new emotion so that it can finish normally without hurting (sinning against) anyone else. You can do that by first admitting to yourself and the other what you are feeling. Do not blame or accuse them; just report to them what you are feeling. Then give yourself a few minutes to let the physical functions finish before going on with the activity or conversation in which you were involved.

Reporting your feelings to others is not all that hard. You must be direct and use "I" messages. Say something like, "I am feeling angry right now. It's not your fault; I just get upset quickly when I hear certain words used. I need a 'time out' so I can settle down."

Surprises at Sunrise Avenue

Sunrise Avenue Community Church had grown rapidly under the effective leadership of Pastor Don. When the membership reached the pastor's saturation point, the board wisely brought in an associate pastor to help him. The secretary's position was upgraded to a full-time position and a part-time youth director/minister of music was hired.

Two years later the youth and education departments were bulging at the seams. A new wing, complete with a recreational area and family center, was constructed. Activities increased, the senior leadership team met weekly and the pastoral staff spent every day and nearly every night in ministry.

Within a short time the youth and music ministries both expanded to full-time positions. In addition to that, a congregational nurture and discipleship staff position was created and the secretarial pool was expanded. The financial strain on the church could be felt, but enthusiasm ran high and attendance continued to increase.

The staff recognized the early warning signs of burnout and implemented better staff meeting designs and group recreational activities. They created small Bible study groups to meet the needs of all major leadership groups and their families. A denominational periodical cited them as one of the most creative and innovative fast-growing churches of the region.

The demands upon the staff and their families created pressures of unsurmounting proportions. Some alleviated the pressures through wholesome and energetic recreational activities. Others developed good group support systems to help them reflect on the changes taking place around them and within them. Still others, because of who they were, became either moody or hypersensitive. Happiness and biblical *shalom* were sacrificed for the "cause of the Kingdom."

A bombshell exploded one day at a staff meeting when a conflict between an associate pastor and the senior pastor broke out into the open. Members of the staff alternately experienced anger, fear and sadness. Within two weeks the entire staff was polarized. It took several months to mend the rift and heal the wounds. During that time ministry development slowed immensely.

Then, just as the joy of spiritual unity was returning, a senior member of the pastoral team shared that he had become emotionally attached to the church organist. He and his wife did not have good communication, he said, nor did they share many common interests. He had found spiritual intimacy discussing the message of the hymns with the organist, but he was scared. He did not want to sin against her, the church, or his wife and family. He needed help.

The senior pastor arranged a meeting for him with the executive committee of the church board for the next day. The executive board then visited with the organist and found that she had enjoyed the visits but did not see them as sexually provocative. However, she feared the repercussions. They also visited with the pastor's wife, who was initially crushed by the disclosure.

Because there had been no sexual activity and the pastor had come forward as soon as he discovered his plight, the executive board decided to encourage the pastor to seek remedial help without placing him on suspension. However, he was to avoid private contacts with other women and reduce his workload. He was also to submit to the supervision of a spiritual oversight team.

The pastoral staff quickly rallied to provide support for the pastor, his entire family, the organist and her family. Small Bible study and support groups were developed for all parties as well as for the children.

Word did leak out, however and Christian counselors were brought in for distraught church members. Some members left the church when they discovered that the pastor would not be leaving his position. Others deplored the situation, but felt that forgiveness and healing were better than compounding the hurts with another act of separation.

The fictional account of Sunrise Community Church's growth and collapse helps us understand several important truths about how emotions affect our lives. The bombshell which exploded in the staff meeting should have been anticipated. In fact, conflict is a normal part of life.

The worst thing about this bombshell is that the staff was operating under the illusion that Christians never get angry. It would have been far better had they recognized the truth about emotions and allowed anger to rise and fall harmlessly around them without taking it personally.

Another realistic approach in dealing with emotions is that whenever life is intensely focused, as was the case in the rapid growth of the church, release must come sometime. It is entirely possible that is what happened in the staff meeting.

The senior pastor had not allowed himself sufficient opportunity for the ventilation of his emotions, so his body finally took over and ventilated for him. Had he simply recognized that fact and apologized for it, the crisis could have been over much more quickly without the long-term effects that the staff experienced.

The long-term effects of the explosion do illustrate, however, what happens in any relationship when protective emotions are not dealt with in the right way. Anger and fear set in and neutralize the energy which is otherwise available for ministry. As persons begin to look out for their own well-being, they have less energy left for ministry. They become apathetic and lethargic and seek survival in maintenance ministries.

Another way to deal with stress is to seek relief by separating ourselves from one of the stressors in our life. This has the positive effect of giving us more energy for other tasks. Unfortunately, we often separate from a task or individual which is not to blame for the major stress factors in our life and thus bring great damage to innocent persons and other important parts of our life.

That is what may have happened with the pastor who became emotionally involved with the organist. It is true that many marriages become stale, but there are many different reasons for that. One is not giving enough attention to developing the relationship in the early years. Another is simply taking the other for granted. It is easy to expect the spouse to read our minds instead of communicating clearly what we are thinking and feeling.

In other cases, however, individuals do genuinely drift apart because their interests are not as compatible as they thought they would be when they first met. Chapter seven outlined many reasons within our personalities which may cause that to happen.

That is not reason enough for abandoning a relationship, however (in a pastor/church relationship as well as in a marital one). Individual differences can enhance our lives and broaden our relationships if we give them a chance. The task before us then is to sit down with the other and talk through the differences in a dispassionate way, seeking ways to enhance the relationship in spite of the differences that may exist.

By now you are probably quite emotionally involved in this discussion. The decision on the part of the senior pastor and the board to take no drastic action with regard to the incident between the associate pastor and the organist no doubt has your full attention. Some of you will applaud the action and others will seriously question it.

I recognize that people will react to this imaginary story in different ways, depending upon their own personal orientation and experience regarding intimate contacts. Some of you will argue that leaders must adhere to a higher standard than others, in which case the pastor should have voluntarily stepped down or been removed from office. Others will argue that there is only one standard which should be applied to everyone equally. Some will argue that the route of forgiveness, love and compassion was the right one to take, while others will insist that no one should be allowed to avoid the consequences of sin.

The important lesson is that in any conflict or crisis, no matter what decision a group makes, it will have to deal with the consequences. In the case of Sunrise Church, some members left the church because of the decision to show mercy, but others would have left if the pastor had been removed from office.

With proper care and guidance the pastor could have healed in or out of office, but removal from office would have been harder on his already broken family system. A church must be ready to deal with the consequences of whatever action it decides to take.

The compassionate way in which the pastoral staff cared for everyone in the two families shows the tender side of the Christian faith. The willingness to bring in outside counselors to help distraught members of the church was also a magnanimous gesture of Christian care.

One thing that would have helped the church immensely would have been a public statement from the board. They could have instructed their chairperson to enunciate the church's clear view regarding inappropiate intimate contacts. At the same time they could have endorsed compassionate care for the persons involved. Giving the reason for certain stances is much better than simply allowing people to second guess what is taking place from rumors and half-truths.

Those members who deplored the situation but stayed anyway illustrate the truth that inflicting a second wound to address the first wound is often not the best solution in dealing with conflict.

Truly, any time an individual departs from a group, an organization, or a family, it leaves a wound. Avoidance or absenteeism is not the best way to deal with a hurt. It is far better to remain with the group, talk things out patiently and carefully and seek the growth of ourselves and others in the process.

This discussion has not attempted to deal with all the complicated realities of sexual sin or indiscretions in high places. Many others have done that already and more efforts will surely follow.[4]

However, this imaginary account of life in the complicated world of today helps to demonstrate how volatile emotions can be. As we said earlier, you have probably experienced your own deep emotion as you read the account and the commentary that followed. What we must learn above all else is that no one is immune to the fragility of his/her emotions. Yet we are all created by God with our emotions. We have the responsibility of learning how to recognize them and manage them appropriately, according to clear Christian values.

---

1. Stanley Keleman, *Emotional Anatomy: The Structure of Experience*, Berkeley, Calif.: Center Press, 1985, pp. xii, 157. Although Keleman's religious stance is unknown to this author, his work is an example of how pure scientific research can help Christians understand more about God's magnificent creation.

2. Dixie Morris and Frank Morris, *Therapeutic Feelings: A Companion for Adventurers*, Arlington Heights, Ill.: Liberation Psychology Training Center (3375 No. Arlington Heights Road, Suites A, B, 60004), 1988. The original research of the Morrises, spanning three decades, included work with children. This work was important because children are so open and genuine in expressing what they feel. [Here also, see the note about pure scientific research above.] David E. Carlson, *Counseling and Self-Esteem*, in Gary R. Collins, gen. ed., Resources for Christian Counseling, Waco, Tex.: Word Books, 1988, chap. 8, "Teaching Counselees to Nurture Themselves Through Recognizing and Accepting Feelings" first brought these concepts to the author's attention.

3. A new emotion is one that comes into being as the result of a new event, action or idea. Whenever an emotion is aroused as the result of past memories, it can easily last much longer. Also, if we choose to nurture an emotion or dwell on any event, action or idea, the emotion can last much longer than eight minutes.

4. See e.g., Karen Lebacqz and Ronald G. Barton, *Sex in the Parish*, Louisville: Westminster/John Knox Press, 1991, for an excellent study with bibliography, funded by the Lilly Foundation; Bill Perkins, "Sex—An American Obsession," *Fatal*

Attractions: Overcoming Our Secret Addictions, Eugene, Ore.: Harvest House, 1991, chapter five; Marlin E. Thomas, "8 Reasons Why Pastors Cross the Boundaries of Sexual Propriety," in *The Christian Leader*, Oct. 8, 1991, pp. 5-6; and Katie Funk Wiebe, "Sex in the Workplace," in *The Marketplace*, Nov/Dec. 1989, pp. 4-9. See also Ellen Hollinger, ed., *Crossing the Boundary: Professional Sexual Abuse Educational Packet*, Akron, Penn.: Mennonite Central Committee U.S. Women's Concerns, 1991, for a very helpful packet of information on dealing with sexual offenses.

PART FOUR

PRACTICE:
HOW TO DEAL WITH
CONFLICT SUCCESSFULLY

CHAPTER NINE

Conflict Management Tools for Servant Leaders

> *Jesus called them together and said, "You know that the rulers of the Gentiles lord it over them and their high officials exercise authority over them. Not so with you. Instead, whoever wants to become great among you must be your servant and whoever wants to be first must be your slave--just as the Son of Man did not come to be served, but to serve and to give his life as a ransom for many"* (Matt 20:25-28).

The title of this chapter ought to suggest immediately that we will not be discussing conflict management or servant leadership in the usual way. When we combine them we encounter a very special opportunity for ministry to people. Before we begin, we need to look at two definitions.

Jesus invited his disciples to shun rank among themselves. Instead, he wanted them to relate to one another as equals or colleagues, to use a modern term. He wanted them to serve one another, thus remaining on equal serving terms with each other.

A servant leader in today's world, then, is one who relates to those s/he serves as equals and colleagues. Pontificating the wisdom of God from a position of superiority is not acceptable to Jesus. He does not allow others to walk all over him, but neither does he walk on any of them. There are definitely times when authoritative leadership is needed, but authoritarianism is never helpful in the church, the family, or the Christian organization.

When such a servant leader enters the arena of group conflict, the entry is as a lifeguard and an emergency medical technician. There is no time for long, technical, collegial discussions. The call at this time is to save lives and ministries.

S/he must exercise responsible leadership which will accomplish the general goals, while also dealing compassionately and gently with those who are drowning. Authoritarianism just does not work, although authoritative leadership is expected and needed.

Decision-making by Consensus

In working with a conflicted system, it is important to help the group develop a better decision-making system. Frequently one reason a group develops destructive conflict is that the decision-making process has degenerated or even disintegrated. It may fall captive to the group's power struggles and degenerate into a pathetic caricature of itself. On the other hand, it may be kidnapped by a minority of persons and simply become an ugly rule by individual fiat.

Servant leadership carefully leads the group to learn how to make decisions by consensus. This approach builds upon the example and teaching of Jesus and his apostles. We can find the best illustrations of how it works in John 4, John 13 and Acts 15.

Servant leadership does not destroy the self-esteem or integrity of other individuals in the group. It does seek, however, the total spiritual, social, emotional and physical well-being of all the people in the church, group or family. It frees up the caring individual so s/he may be more fully the person God has called him/her to be. Servant leadership also legitimizes the individuality and viewpoint of all the persons with whom one must live and work.

That does not mean that leading by consensus is easy. On the contrary, it is hard. For one thing, it is contrary to human nature. For another, it calls for more patience and tact than many people care to develop. Further, in our rapidly advancing technological age, it is more difficult than it ever has been in the past because not everyone can keep up equally well with changing ways of thinking and doing things.

However, with the multitude of people problems and ecological issues which we encounter today, we do not have many other options. We must learn how to get along with each other better, or we will truly all self-destruct.

Free to Serve as a Servant

One way a Christian, servant leader may free him/herself to serve others more adequately is by observing the six basic principles for successful living. They were mentioned already in chapter seven, but will be repeated here with brief elaborations.

"I can live with that."

Consensus is a beautiful thing!

1. Give life permission to be just the way it is. There are many things in life that you just cannot change. Learning to live with reality is better than spoiling all of life by constantly seeking perfection. The Serenity Prayer may help accomplish this goal.

2. Be who you are—responsibly. The one thing you can control is how you behave. Live by the principles which you believe are right. That way God will not judge you as delinquent of your primary responsibility. Let your light shine for others to see, but let them accept it as they are able.

3. Let others be who they are—caringly. You can only encourage others; you cannot force them. Show Christian care to those who do not have the same light as you do and pray for the day when you both will mature in your spirits. Until then, do not begrudge them your love and friendship.

4. Be willing to say where you are—kindly. Do not expect others to read your mind. Tell them carefully, lovingly and in a straightforward manner what is important to you and how you want to live. Feel free to tell them when you agree and disagree, but do so kindly.

5. Let others say where they are—acceptingly. Be willing also to listen to what others say about themselves. You may not agree with them, but accept them as being on the road of life just as you are. Remember that in God's own time he will bring everyone to maturity (Phil. 3:15-16).

6. Care about your sister and brother—appropriately. While your sister or brother is on the way, show them true Christian love and care. Forgive their mistakes and overlook those you cannot forgive. Be their friend, not their God. Wait until they come to you for advice and then give it as a fellow pilgrim, not as the authority of authorities.

The indented paragraphs above are designed to show conceptual relationships among the six principles. Thus paragraphs 1 and 6 are equal in terms of emphasis, as are paragraphs 2 and 3 and 4 and 5. Paragraphs 2 and 3 represent one unit of thought and paragraphs 4 and 5 represent a parallel unit of thought. Paragraphs 1-3 form a unit of being, while paragraphs 4-6 form a unit of doing.

Applying Biblical Principles in a Modern Era

How can we apply the principles of Jesus and the apostles to the church, Christian group, or family of today? We first must remember that we are not living in the pioneer era of the first century. It is not necessary to develop a brand new church organism from scratch. Neither is it necessary to develop a brand new understanding of the family as a Christian unit, as was true in the New Testament era. Refinements sometimes are necessary, but wholesale redesigning is not.

We must remember that none of the churches to which Paul wrote had been established for longer than twenty years. When the New Testament canon closed, no group of believers had more than two generations of experience in following Christ. There were no Christian organizations other than Paul's missionary organization.

It is different today. Many of our churches are seasoned, well-established churches; many of our Christian families have been immersed in biblical training for decades. Many of our fine Christian organizations have had excellent precursors and are wonderful role models for newer organizations.

Pastors, Christian CEOs, supervisors and parents who come to their responsibilities as if there was nothing but chaos before they arrived will not serve their charges well. It is not necessary to reinvent the wheel. We must hear the words of the apostle Paul in Philippians 3:15-16 and continue to move on toward greater maturity.

There are many areas in which we can move beyond the past. The New Testament does not anticipate every detailed iota with which we are confronted today. For example, neither Jesus nor Paul wrote a church constitution for us. They did not develop organizational flow charts or discuss the fine points of joint parenting. Those were things better left to succeeding generations. They knew that each generation of believers would have to figure out some things for themselves. Doing that peacefully, however, is not a simple task.

Four Steps for Leadership in a Conflict Situation[1]

Active Listening

The first step in developing a servant leader approach for conflict management, in the church or anywhere else, is learning how to listen actively to everyone's point of view. That is illustrated abundantly in Acts 15:1-12, where everyone involved in the controversy had an equal opportunity to speak and the whole assembly listened carefully to them.

Active listening is different from ordinary listening. Most of the time we listen passively, waiting for the other to finish so we can talk. We turn on our ears but our eyes wander about the room. Our hands fidget with our papers and we shuffle our feet or cross our legs. We may even try to keep in touch with other sounds in the room.

Active listening is empathetic listening. We tune out other sounds and give the speaker good eye contact. We nod our head. We show agreement or disagreement or at least a sense of understanding with little grunts and squeals. There is light in our eyes as we connect with the emotion of the speaker. Our body language is focused on the other. We show in myriad ways that we are fully attentive to the other's concern.[2]

In learning how to practice active listening in churches, Christian groups and families, it is important to remember four points.

1. Fear is the first enemy to be overcome if everyone is to be heard. Some people, based upon their previous experiences, may fear that no one will take them seriously. Others may fear negative criticism. Still others may fear outright rejection or the hurt of being ignored later, after having courageously spoken their mind.

Some people may fear public ridicule or even physical abuse. It takes lots and lots of patient, careful listening to overcome repeated experiences of a loss of credibility and power. For example, it took five tries for Jesus to get the woman at the well of Sychar to approach the core of her inner being (John 4).

Finally, some fear their own negative emotions. They may feel emotions stirring within them, but may not know how to release them unless servant leaders can make it safe for them.

2. Second, it is important to listen with equal ears to everyone in the group. Quiet, reserved persons speak up less quickly than do outgoing, gregarious persons. Those at the lower end of the power structure may not even bother speaking unless a caring servant leader helps them feel that they really do count.

That rule is also true for the weakest member of a family circle and for the one in the group who always has a different idea. That differentness does not make them wrong; it just makes them feel awkward. Active listening helps them to overcome their fears. It also makes it possible for more outspoken members of the family or group to hear them — maybe for the first time.

3. Third, active listening must legitimize each person in the group as a person in his/her own right. In boards and committees and even in congregations and conferences, it is easy to quickly begin working on the agenda of the more vocal and energetic persons in the group. That approach ignores the deep-seated feelings and thoughts of those in the group who are more quiet.

Servant leaders who really care must learn how to call forth the views of the less powerful and the minorities in the group. Pastors must find a balance between accomplishing their goals for the church and freeing up the people for ministry according to their God-given insights and gifts. Parents and siblings must both learn to enjoy walking along the trail with each other. They need to avoid lecturing each other about doing what they are not yet ready to do.

4. Fourth, it is important to attend both to the facts and to the feelings surrounding each issue being discussed. It is hard enough to sort out all of the different ideas which may develop in a good round-table discussion. It is even harder to become aware of the myriad of feelings that surround those ideas. It is hardest of all to be in touch with the feelings within oneself which often threaten to short-circuit the listening process. First it is important to learn how to listen to different ideas. Then we must learn how to attend both to our feelings and those of others involved in the conversation.

Perceptions Clarification

The second step in developing a servant leader approach to conflict management is that of perceptions clarification. Perceptions clarification is distinguishing clearly between each person's different feelings and ideas concerning the issues before the group.

That step is not illustrated in Acts 15 but it is more clearly in view in Acts 6. There both the apostles and the lay leaders clearly paid attention to the feelings of the frustrated widows. In Acts 15 the feelings of the Christian "traditionalists" were not adequately processed. That is one reason, I believe, why Paul had to deal with the issue again in 1 Corinthians 8 and Romans 14-15.

In other words, the conservative Christians, originally trained as Pharisees, really were not as comfortable with the compromise as they could have been. On the other hand, Paul was not as comfortable with the "eating meat offered to idols" section of the agreement. Later he discarded that part of the compromise.

In coming to understand perceptions clarification, it is again necessary to make four points.

1. First, it is important to ask the right questions. As much confusion is generated by asking the wrong questions as by jumping to hasty conclusions.

As a person begins sorting out the many individual facts from a multitude of confused feelings, it is important to ask simple, short objective questions. As we suggested earlier, the news reporter's five "W" questions plus "How" will work quite well. The question "Why" should not be included because it slows the process of getting at the hard-core facts. That question should wait until much later, or be omitted entirely.

In seeking to clarify perceptions it is important to get the details right. It is helpful to remember Whitehead's dictum that "we live in specifics, but we speak in generalities." It is also important to give attention to each person's version of the issue and to help people get all the facts straight.

2. Second, it is important to avoid making assumptions when trying to clarify perceptions. It is easy for pastors, moderators, congregational chairs and board and committee chairs to make hasty assumptions about people's intentions. It is also easy for family members and friends to do the same about each other.

You do not really know what a person is thinking or feeling or wanting until they tell you. They may not be able to tell you everything they want to say the first time you ask, so you must keep listening and asking. Helping people clarify perceptions for themselves, for you and for others in the group is part of the task of serving God in a conflicted group.

3. Third, it is important to be aware of the three filters of communication (see page 133). It is important to help people understand the difference between the way they perceive something, the way you perceive something and the way the open space between both of you changes the meaning of information.

It is also important to help them understand that any time another person is introduced into the relationship, the filtering factor is at least cubed in complexity. That means communication must slow down and become much more intentional in order for meaning to flow adequately.

MODEL OF COMMUNICATION

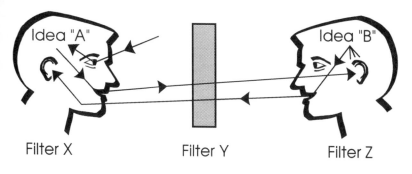

Filter X   Filter Y   Filter Z

"A" represents an idea the person on the left wants to communicate to the person on the right. Filter "X" in the speaker causes him to tell only what he chooses to tell about it. "Z," an internal filter in the receiver of the message, filters out still more before the idea is received by the person on the right. Filter "Y" represents external factors between the speaker and the listener that alter the communciation. Thus idea "A" is changed into idea "B" which represents what finally came through to the receiver. This model of communication will give us some idea of the complexity of communication.

4. Fourth, it is important to understand the priority of empathy over sympathy in helping people sort out their problems. It is also better to utilize it at this stage instead of at Step One in the communication process.

Sympathy is "feeling the same hurt with" someone in their pain or disappointment; empathy is "feeling sorry because of a hurt" that another person experienced. It is not as helpful to the hurt person if the caregiver hurts at the same time or in the same way as that person. That only clouds judgment at a time when clear thinking is sorely needed. For example, if John is hurting because Fred attacked him in a board meeting, that attack probably hurt Sam also. Sam could sympathize, but he could not be an objective, empathetic caregiver for John.

It is important, however, for the caregiver's sensitivities to allow him/her to take seriously the concerns of the other. It is also important to let the other person feel that his/her concerns truly occupy center stage on the caregiver's agenda.

A person who was not hurt by Fred's comment can empathize with John and help him work through his feelings much more objectively than Sam could. It is better to do that here at the perceptions clarification stage after everyone has had a chance to speak at least once in the active listening stage. If it comes too early in the listening process each person's viewpoint cannot be legitimized with enough awareness and clarity.

Teaching How to Build Better Relationships

The third step in a servant leader approach to conflict management is that of teaching people in conflict how to build better relationships with each other. There is abundant biblical support for such an effort, beginning with Romans 12:9-21 and Philippians 2:1-4. In seeking to develop more fully the content of those and other scriptures, it is well to observe several rules of good teaching.

The first is the priority of teaching over advising. There is a great difference between the two. It has often been said that it is possible to preach without an audience present, but it is impossible to teach without willing students.

We can carry that one step farther. Teaching does not really occur until people discover how they can make better decisions for themselves. Advice, on the other hand, offers a specific suggestion for a specific problem at a specific time. It is often invaluable in a crunch; it is seldom helpful in the long run.

The best teaching cannot occur until the teacher knows something about the student as well as the subject matter. Furthermore, the best learning cannot occur until the students can trust the teacher with some of their personal, secret needs.

After the patient, caring servant leader has given adequate attention to Step One, listening carefully to each person in the conflict and to Step Two, seeking to help each person in the group clarify their perceptions about the issues at stake, a context for life-changing instruction emerges much more clearly.

The leader then has a better understanding of each person's position, exactly what they need to learn and how much new learning they can accept. Then the remaining temptation is to finish the lesson too quickly. It is better to move patiently and slowly enough so each step in the learning process is adequately developed.

One of the first things that a Christian caregiver must teach others is the art of good listening (Phil. 2:4). Persons in conflict must learn how to choose to listen. Then they must learn how to listen actively. They must learn how to differentiate in their listening between facts, ideas and feelings and they must begin to give attention to body language. They must also learn how to listen to themselves.

Another thing servant leaders must teach conflicted persons and groups is how to talk together better (Eph. 4:25). They must learn how to choose their words so people will understand what they want to get across. They must learn how to deliver positive messages and how not to overload the listening circuits. They must also learn to give attention to the persons to whom they are speaking and speak with respect and courtesy.

A third item to teach persons in conflict is how to develop for themselves the skills of perceptions clarification. They need to learn how to say, "The way I see it is . . ." instead of "This is the way it is." They also need to learn how to ask each other, "What does this issue look like to you?" rather than "You have it all wrong."

They need to understand that although all truth is God's truth, none of us possesses all of it. They need to be encouraged to recognize that in some situations there is more than one "right" way to solve a problem.

Finally, teach people in conflict to be permission givers (see chapter eight). Because on average, 77% of people's thoughts are negative (chapter one), lots of learning needs to take place so people can say "Yes" to other people more easily. There certainly are moral absolutes in life which must be defended. However, we do not spend most of our time defending those moral absolutes. Most of the time our lives have to do with the practical, day-to-day chores of living and there must be more room for flexibility there.

Spending most of our life with the "nuts and bolts" of living is just as true for churches as it is for families and for other groups. Life is lived mostly in the realm of goals and methods.

There are many good methods by which to accomplish the goals which make life worthwhile. God gives the gift of good ideas to many people.

Empowerment

The fourth step in a servant leader approach to conflict management is that of developing a process of empowerment for each other. This process should help people feel good about doing what they believe God is calling them to do. The process can begin by helping them negotiate the best solution possible for their conflicts. It should also help them deal both with the feelings and the ideas of all the people in the group. For this we can return to Acts 15, where verses 13-29 show an attempt to do just that.

We must remember, however, that this type of collaborative decision making takes time to develop. It may be less efficient for the rapid organizational development of the church program. However, the alternative of making decisions by too-hasty votes or calling for minority compliance destroys the spiritual unity of the group which Christ died to attain (John 17).

We can empower people in groups to do the work God has called them to do by following these four rules:

1. First, help people differentiate between decisions about themselves and decisions about others. One of the greatest temptations we face is trying to make decisions about how other people should live their lives. There is always plenty of room for negotiating differences. However, people who wish to manage their conflicts better must learn that it is wrong to presume upon other persons.

Take the Sunday school teacher who wants fifteen minutes of playtime each class period. A problem arises if s/he wants the other teacher to help with it, or even to direct it, when the other teacher is not ready to do it. In such a case the first teacher must be willing to wait or to direct it alone.

Or take the case where one or two board members want to change the time of a meeting for the sake of personal convenience. That is no problem if the other board members can agree. But if they do not all agree to the change, those who want to change the schedule should exercise tolerance. They should rearrange their own schedules to alleviate the problem.

Another example is one family member wanting to experience a part of life differently from the usual family pattern. S/he should not presume singlehandedly upon everyone else in the family to grant them his/her wish.

2. Second, empowerment comes more readily when people can be helped to make appropriate decisions for and about themselves. Not everyone in church must agree to something before one person may seek it for him/herself.

If one person or family chooses to skip the Sunday school picnic, that does not necessarily mean they have no interest in Sunday school. Again, if one couple chooses to invite a new family out for Sunday dinner, that does not mean they are disloyal to their friends.

An individual who feels strongly that it is time to make some personal changes in his/her life should be encouraged to do so on the basis of God's will, not on the basis of what others might say or think. Wise counsel is one thing; manipulative peer pressure is quite another. Only in making personal decisions appropriately will people discover the power to do the will of God in the freedom of Christ.

3. Third, the process of empowerment moves forward when people become willing to let others make decisions for and about themselves which they believe are right for them. It is important to learn how to say "Yes" to others without first having to decide if it is acceptable for them.

Some decisions about life and ministry simply are not in the public domain, as important as the life of the body may be. For example, starting a Sunday school class for recent newcomers or painting the trim in the nursery is not necessarily a spiritual decision which the whole church or even a few favorite leaders in the church need to make.

4. A fourth and final rule to remember in helping people become empowered for better living and ministry is that the process of empowerment takes time. It also involves more ingredients than those which have been mentioned here. Much could be said about the role of prayer, meditation and Bible study in empowering people for Christian living and ministry. Much could also be said concerning the work of God in our lives through the ministry of the Holy Spirit. What we have tried to do here is to touch a few areas of life that are often otherwise untouched when we think about managing our conflicts.

At the beginning of this chapter we suggested that the greatest issue within persons when dealing with conflict is fear.

On the other hand, pride and impatience may be the last feelings to be overcome. We must be willing to live our lives with respect to other persons differently, more openly and with more respect and courtesy for them.

It is important to help conflicted people in our congregations, parachurch organizations and families develop appropriate power in their own lives. This is true both in their private lives and in their public ministries.

To do so we must be willing to revise our priorities in ministry so that we give enough time to empowering the whole body of Christ. God will take care of the program of ministry in the church. I believe God calls his servants to serve the people under their care. I believe God calls us first to build up the body of Christ and only then to enlarge the tents.

---

1. See Marlin E. Thomas, "The Pastor's Role in Managing Church Conflict," *Direction*, 19:2 (Fall 1990), pp. 65-74.

2. See e.g., Paul W. Swets, "Learn the Listening Art," in *The Art of Talking So That People Will Listen*, New York: Prentice Hall, 1983 chapter four.

3. Willard Claassen, *Learning to Lead*, Scottdale, Penn.: Herald Press, 1963, p. 41.

CHAPTER TEN

Conflict Management in a Committee Meeting: A Role Play

This chapter is designed to give you an opportunity to practice what you have learned so far. It will also help teach more effective ways of conducting a committee meeting by practicing both behavior patterns.

The basic types of persons in the committee are a composite of chapters four, six and seven. The conflict levels which you may encounter are reviewed in chapters one, two, three and eight. The principles which you may apply in resolving conflicts are found in chapters five and nine.

You may make assignments for each part in the role play in advance or at the time the role play is staged. If you choose this latter approach, give each player enough time to read through their part so they are not embarrassed during the role play. The group leader may make the assignments, or group participants may volunteer for parts.

PERMISSION IS HEREBY GRANTED TO MAKE PHOTOCOPIES OF THE PAGES IN THIS CHAPTER ONLY FOR THE EXPRESS PURPOSE OF STAGING THE ROLE PLAY and ONLY IF ALL PLAYERS DO NOT HAVE ACCESS TO COPIES OF THE BOOK.

If possible, we suggest that you observe the following guidelines in setting up the role play.
1. The leader or teacher of the group should serve as the moderator of this learning exercise, or secure an individual to fill that role. The moderator shall make sure that everyone who plays a part fully understands their role. S/he shall explain to the audience (if there is one) that the players are performing roles and not necessarily portraying themselves. The leader shall also explain that discussion times will be included following each role play. S/he shall read the **Setting** and **Agenda Item** to the audience before the role play begins. S/he shall also explain that each role play episode will begin where the other one left off.

139

2. There will be three separate episodes, each presided over by a different chairperson. Each chair will work from five to ten minutes, depending upon how much time is available.

3. There will be four committee members plus the pastor (optional), each sitting in on all three meetings of the role play.

4. The committee members should include the following categories if possible:

   a. An older person.

   b. A younger person.

   c. At least two women (may serve as chair/s if desired).

5. At the end of each episode the moderator should allow time for discussion. Following are some items which may be covered.

   a. Allow each participant to say how s/he experienced the meeting.

      i. Positive and negative feelings.

      ii. Unanswered questions about the procedures.

      iii. What they would have done differently.

      iv. What they really liked about the procedures.

   b. Allow members of the audience to say how they perceived the meeting.

      i. Positive and negative feelings.

      ii. Unanswered questions about the procedures.

      iii. What they would have done differently.

      iv. What they really liked about the procedures.

6. At the end of each discussion period allow the chairperson to identify the assigned profile, or to read it if the audience does not have access to copies of the book.

7. After all three discussions have finished, allow each of the committee members to identify their assignment profiles, or read them if the audience does not have access to copies of the book.

ROLE PLAY: CONFLICT MANAGEMENT IN A COMMITTEE MEETING

Chairperson (#1)

Setting: As a result of a decision at the annual congregational meeting last month, the church board has convened a special committee to study a recommendation for community evangelism. The committee is broadly based, including both women and men, young and old, leadership types and those not in leadership. Everyone knows each other. This is the first meeting of the committee.

Agenda Item: At the annual church meeting last month the congregation passed a motion to broadcast the Sunday morning worship service over the local Cable TV network in order to reach more people.

Role: Chairperson, playing the *Competitive* style of conflict management.

1. You open the meeting by saying, "Well, you all know what we're here for. Now, I've done a little preliminary research and here's how I think is the best way to proceed."

2. The following is a suggested script. You may develop your own interpretation of it.

   a. "We should buy a new Yamaha camcorder from New Ventures, Inc. of Chicago (or any large city near you). It's the best deal for the money."

   b. "Then we should secure volunteer operators for the equipment on Sunday mornings. Any questions?"

3. Whenever someone on the committee agrees with you or makes a suggestion that is compatible with your idea, encourage that person and endorse his/her efforts. When others reply that they do not agree with the proposal, you ignore them.

4. Whenever someone on the committee raises a question about the proposal which requires study or debate, discount the idea and also sometimes the person.

5. Your goal for this meeting is to get agreement for bringing a representative of New Ventures, Inc. to town for a demonstration. You want to set that up for the next meeting in thirty days.

ROLE PLAY: CONFLICT MANAGEMENT IN A COMMITTEE MEETING

Chairperson (#2)

Setting: As a result of a decision at the annual congregational meeting last month, the church board has convened a special committee to study a recommendation for community evangelism. The committee is broadly based, including both women and men, young and old, leadership types and those not in leadership. Everyone knows each other. This is the second meeting of the committee.

Agenda Item: At the congregational meeting last month a motion was passed to broadcast the Sunday morning worship service over the local Cable TV network in order to reach more people.

Role: Chairperson, playing the *Accommodating* style of conflict management.

1. You take over the meeting by saying, "Well, we did a pretty good job at our last meeting. Now we really need to get down to brass tacks. What are your thoughts now?"

2. Then you basically sit back and let the conversation flow.

3. Whenever someone says something positive, you agree with them and tell them how good their idea is.

4. Whenever someone raises a question or objection, you agree that they have a valid point.

5. If someone seems to be unsure of themselves, you point out that it may be too soon for a decision.

6. If someone seems to be impatient and pushes for a decision, you ask if people are ready to vote.

ROLE PLAY: CONFLICT MANAGEMENT IN A COMMITTEE MEETING

Chairperson (#3)

(This role needs some advance preparation in order to fully accomplish the assignment.)

Setting: As a result of a decision at the annual congregational meeting last month, the church board has convened a special committee to study a recommendation for community evangelism. The committee is broadly based, including both women and men, young and old, leadership types and those not in leadership. Everyone knows each other. This is the third meeting of the committee.

Agenda Item: At the congregational meeting last month a motion was passed to broadcast the Sunday morning worship service over the local Cable TV network in order to reach more people.

Role: Chairperson, playing the *Collaborative* style of conflict management.

1. You begin by summarizing the progress of the two previous meetings. Be very careful here to bring out the positive points that have been covered so far. Also bring out unresolved issues in a positive manner without demeaning any persons.
2. Then you suggest the decision-making steps which might be accomplished next. This will depend in part upon the first two meetings.
   a. Issues which should be understood by now include:
      i. What are the specific reasons for broadcasting the morning services over our local Cable TV network?
      ii. What are the obstacles which we may encounter?
      iii. In what ways can these obstacles be overcome?
      iv. How do each of the members really feel about the proposal? (It is more important to have a clear understanding of feelings than to have unanimity. Differences of opinion are healthy for good decision making.)
   b. If any of the above issues are not resolved, go back and discuss them. Ask all persons to state their views or

opinions, thank them for sharing and go on to the next person. Tell them that what they have just shared will be important in knowing how to carry out the wishes of the congregation.

   c. If and when the above issues are clearly understood (agreement is not necessary), go on with the decision-making process.

3. Decision-making in this setting includes the following steps:

   a. Decide together what specific item/s must be discussed and resolved before the committee can go on.

   b. Resolve the specific issue/s by:

      i. Collecting all the relevant facts and feelings from each person.

      ii. Allowing each person to state his/her position on that specific issue.

      iii. Negotiating whatever differences might remain.

      iv. Agreeing on how to carry out that specific decision.

   c. Move on to identify all the other issues that must be resolved before the broadcast plan can be brought to the church for final action.

ROLE PLAY: CONFLICT MANAGEMENT IN A COMMITTEE MEETING

Member of the committee (#1)

Setting: As a result of a decision at the annual congregational meeting last month, the church board has convened a special committee to study a recommendation for community evangelism. The committee is broadly based, including both women and men, young and old, leadership types and those not in leadership. Everyone knows each other.

The committee will meet three times (three separate role play segments), each time with a different style chairperson. There will be a short break between each meeting segment. Members of the committee will be asked to describe how they felt about each segment.

Agenda Item: At the congregational meeting last month a motion was passed to broadcast the Sunday morning worship service over the local Cable TV network in order to reach more people.

Role: Member of the committee.

1. You are basically *against* new proposals and ideas.
2. You can usually see the dangers and problems of new ventures and you try to make other people see your point of view.
3. You are not really against the pastor and other leadership individuals, but you worry about all the new ideas they bring into the life of the church. It does not make sense to change things too often.
4. You were among those who voiced intelligent opposition to this new proposal at the congregational meeting and when the church board asked you to serve on this committee, you agreed out of a sense of commitment to the church.

ROLE PLAY: CONFLICT MANAGEMENT
IN A COMMITTEE MEETING

Member of the committee (#2)

Setting: As a result of a decision at the annual congregational meeting last month, the church board has convened a special committee to study a recommendation for community evangelism. The committee is broadly based, including both women and men, young and old, leadership types and those not in leadership. Everyone knows each other.

The committee will meet three times (three separate role play segments), each time with a different style chairperson. There will be a short break between each meeting segment. Members of the committee will be asked to describe how they felt about each segment.

Agenda Item: At the congregational meeting last month a motion was passed to broadcast the Sunday morning worship service over the local Cable TV network in order to reach more people.

Role: Member of the committee.

1. You always *back the chairperson* of any committee on which you serve.
2. You are relatively new in the church (about eight years) and you would like to be on the church board some day. You try hard to be a "good team player."
3. You do not like to "rock the boat" of a committee and you get nervous when anyone else does.
4. You have your own reasons for feeling the way you do about this resolution and you try sincerely to participate in the discussion.

ROLE PLAY: CONFLICT MANAGEMENT IN A COMMITTEE MEETING

Member of the committee (#3)

Setting: As a result of a decision at the annual congregational meeting last month, the church board has convened a special committee to study a recommendation for community evangelism. The committee is broadly based, including both women and men, young and old, leadership types and those not in leadership. Everyone knows each other.

The committee will meet three times (three separate role play segments), each time with a different style chairperson. There will be a short break between each meeting. Members of the committee will be asked to describe how they felt about each meeting.

Agenda Item: At the congregational meeting last month a motion was passed to broadcast the Sunday morning worship service over the local Cable TV network in order to reach more people.

Role: Member of the committee.

1. You have a *hard time making up your mind.*
2. You have your own opinions about this proposal, but you do not want to antagonize anyone. Conflict is hard for you to handle.
3. You are really a likeable person and find it easy to be friends with everyone. You can also see the good points in almost everything committee members say.
4. The task of discussing pros and cons of an issue is difficult for you. You would like to come to a good decision soon and get on with life with enjoying your friends and family in a more relaxed atmosphere.

ROLE PLAY: CONFLICT MANAGEMENT IN A COMMITTEE MEETING

Member of the committee (#4)

Setting: As a result of a decision at the annual congregational meeting last month, the church board has convened a special committee to study a recommendation for community evangelism. The committee is broadly based, including both women and men, young and old, leadership types and those not in leadership. Everyone knows each other.

The committee will meet three times (three separate role play segments), each time with a different style chairperson. There will be a short break between each meeting segment. Members of the committee will be asked to describe how they felt about each meeting.

Agenda Item: At the congregational meeting last month a motion was passed to broadcast the Sunday morning worship service over the local Cable TV network, in order to reach more people.

Role: Member of the committee.

1. You are generally *in favor of every new idea.*
2. You are dedicated to the idea that the church should remain fresh, modern and up-to-date. The church cannot afford to lag behind the rest of society.
3. You are generally supportive of the pastor, the chair of your committee and others on the committee who have good ideas.
4. You were one of the people in the congregation who pushed for this project.

ROLE PLAY: CONFLICT MANAGEMENT IN A COMMITTEE MEETING

Member of the committee, ex officio as pastor.

Setting: As a result of a decision at the annual congregational meeting last month, the church board has convened a special committee to study a recommendation for community evangelism. The committee is broadly based, including both women and men, young and old, leadership types and those not in leadership. Everyone knows each other.

The committee will meet three times (three separate role play segments), each time with a different style chairperson. There will be a short break between each meeting segment. Members of the committee will be asked to describe how they felt about each segment.

Agenda Item: At the congregational meeting last month a motion was passed to broadcast the Sunday morning worship service over the local Cable TV network in order to reach more people.

Role: Pastor of the church; ex officio member of the committee.

1. You serve this committee purely in *an advisory capacity*.
2. You have had some experience in broadcasting church services and you know the benefits as well as the pitfalls.
3. You listen to the discussion and comment occasionally when the discussion begins to get off track.
4. Although some members of the committee expect you to serve as an answer man, you remain totally neutral, allowing the committee to own fully the project.

CHAPTER ELEVEN

The Fine Art of Mediation:
Three Case Studies[1]

We already discussed Matthew 18:15-20 in chapters three and five. In this chapter we want to move beyond a theological discussion to present a technique that really works.

There is one word of caution before we begin. Talking theoretically about a Scripture passage or even talking in theory about a mediation technique differs from actually mediating a disagreement or conflict. The one variable which is difficult to control is the emotions of the people involved.

If you want to take Matthew 5:23-24 and 18:15 seriously, your own emotions will play a significant part in the encounter. The emotions of the other party will also be significant. If you want to put Matthew 18:16 into effect, your emotions, as well as the emotions of the other party and the two or three witnesses, will be involved.

This is one important reason we discussed the role of emotions in chapter eight. All the theology in the world will not suffice if you are not keenly in touch with your own emotions. It is also important for you to be aware of the emotions of all the other members involved in the encounter.

Matthew 5:23-24 or 18:15

"Therefore, if you are offering your gift at the altar and there remember that your brother has something against you, leave your gift there in front of the altar. First go and be reconciled to your brother; then come and offer your gift" (Matt. 5:23-24).

"If your brother sins against you, go and show him his fault, just between the two of you. If he listens to you, you have won your brother over" (Matt. 18:15).

Offended people often spend a lot of time debating who has the responsibility of apologizing first. It really does not matter. Jesus teaches that either party may take the initiative. Actually, the one whose conscience is touched by the Holy Spirit should not wait for the other.

There are four steps in a healthy mediation process. The first is reporting the facts and the feelings to the other as you have experienced them. Do not resort to blaming. Use "I" messages, clearly letting the other person know what the situation was like from your point of view.

Some ways of beginning are:

"Sue, I was upset by what you said. I want to tell you my side of what happened, so we can compare notes and find agreement on it."

"Don, what you did hurt me. Maybe you didn't mean it, but I want to tell you what it felt like to me so we can clear it up before it gets worse."

You will notice that in both cases the speaker takes responsibility for personal feelings and their own personal viewpoint regarding the facts. Accusations and lectures are not acceptable because of the danger of starting another round of conflict.

The second step is for the second party to repeat or paraphrase what the first person has said. This second step is very important. If the second party begins immediately to make excuses or outright denials, another argument could very easily occur.

Some ways of accomplishing this second step in the light of the examples offered above are:

Sue: "I'm sorry, Sally. I didn't mean to upset you. Please tell me how you saw it."

Sally: "I heard you say that Jane didn't want to sing if I was singing and that's not what she told me."

Sue: "Jane didn't tell you the reason she wasn't singing was because you were singing? What did she tell you?"

Don: "I'm sorry, Bill. I didn't mean to hurt you. Please tell me how it felt to you."

Bill: "When I saw you step forward to take the offering in my place, I just felt as if I didn't count at all."

Don: "I can understand how low that made you feel, Bill. Actually, I didn't see you anywhere and I thought you were still on vacation. I'll be more observant next time and again, I'm sorry."

Notice that Sue and Don both express their sorrow over their friends' hurt feelings. They recognize that they did not intend to hurt their friends but their friends were hurt anyway.

For that they are sad and they say so. They also identify with the feelings of the other. That makes it possible for the offended party to let the hurt feelings go.

The third step is not necessary in the above examples, but in more complicated cases it is absolutely essential. That is the step of review (perceptions clarification). Sometimes the hurt occurs in the midst of a long and complicated activity, such as a board meeting or a full evening's activity. For some people, the review will have to include all the steps leading up to the offensive action and all the feelings they felt afterwards.

If this third step is necessary, it is important to accomplish two goals. First, the parties must each clarify all the perceptions and assumptions which surround the issue. Second, they must not stay in that cycle forever, but move on to identify the main issues which need to be settled.

Then comes the fourth step. That is the step of actually resolving the differences. Some people enjoy rehashing the problem more than they do finishing it and putting it behind them. Resolution of the problem may include apologies from both parties. It may also include compromises, confessions and accommodations. Sometimes collaboration makes it possible to find a solution that each one can own fully, so there is no loss felt on either side.

Matthew 18:16

"But if he will not listen, take one or two others along, so that every matter may be established by the testimony of two or three witnesses" (Matt. 18:16).

In a narrow sense, the wording of this text implies that actual damage has occurred and reparations of damage are in order. Thus the two or three witnesses are for the purpose of helping the offender face the offense and reporting back to the church (v. 17) if there is no resolution.

Mediation goes a step farther than that. It seeks to heal the breach between two parties with fair and just solutions for both sides. For that reason, it is right for each party to have its own witness and for both parties to agree on the third neutral mediator.

In some cases the two principle parties may each pick their own witness. Those two witnesses then pick a third which they judge to be neutral and capable of helping to resolve the problem evenhandedly.

Before such a mediation process begins, the neutral person (or persons) should meet with each offended party separately. The purposes for these meetings are to provide a neutral setting in which to hear the facts as each party understands them and also to understand the feelings which are involved.

Those initial meetings are also useful for establishing rapport between the mediator and the offended parties and for laying down the basic ground rules. Both sides must be able to agree individually to all the ground rules before they come together for the mediation session.

The essential ground rules include:
1. The third-party mediator shall be in control of the entire mediation session.
2. If things get out of hand either the mediator or any other party can call a time out.
3. Each party will have equal opportunity to speak.
4. Each party must be willing to listen fully to what the other says.
5. Both parties must understand the four steps in the mediation process:

   a. Report facts and feelings.

   b. Repeat what the other says and feels.

   c. Review unclear elements of the issue until there is unity and clarity on both sides.

   d. Resolve the differences so life can go on in a fair and just manner.

6. Both parties will commit to drawing up and signing an agreement of resolution and will accept guidance from the "two or three others" in coming to full compliance.

Following are two examples of mediation which followed these steps and succeeded in accomplishing the goals of the individuals involved. The names and some elements of each situation have been changed, but the essence of each mediation remains intact. All primary parties consented to the following narrations.

Restoring a Separated Couple

When Lea and Loren came in for counseling, they had already been separated for several months. They had two small children and still loved each other. However, some bad things had happened between them and living together was more painful than either could endure.

Report

Repeat

Review

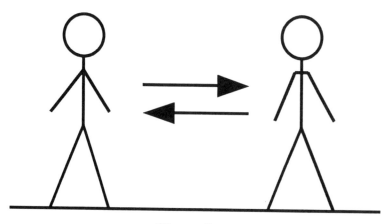

Resolve

During the first session with Loren it became apparent that he had already tried to make amends and was ready to go on. After two more sessions he was ready to return home, but Lea was not ready for that. He came in three more times to process the intense pain of his loneliness.

Lea was stuck with the awful pain of the past several years. She was unable to get past it. She was also not able to negotiate assertively with Loren for a just resolution of her needs. I suggested a joint mediation session and she agreed.

I explained the rules of mediation to her and then met again with Loren to do the same. When the day for mediation came, I suggested that each party sit on opposite sides of the table, across from each other.

I again reviewed the rules and reviewed the agreement that each had made with me earlier. I said there would be two practice sessions before getting into the real issues. Each would be able to speak first in one of those practice sessions. In all cases, they were to look at each other with good eye contact and pay careful attention to body language and each other's feelings.

Loren spoke first. He looked into Lea's eyes and said, "I'm lonely." Lea looked back at him and said, "You're lonely." Loren responded, "Yes, I'm lonely." After two or three more statements by each, I called time.

Then it was Lea's turn to begin. She looked at Loren and said, "I've been thinking about buying a house." Loren looked startled and said, "A house! Which one do you want?" Lea told him and then also explained why. Loren then raised one problem he saw in buying a house at that time and also said how they might be able to work it out. The conversation continued for several minutes. The communication impasse had been broken.

Finally I looked at both of them and said, "Are there any other issues you wish to discuss today?" Both said there were no other issues. Lea came back for two more individual sessions. Some time later I learned that Lea had allowed Loren to move back in and they were doing very well together.

A Visitation Rights Mediation

Adam called me one day and said he had heard that I did mediations. He said he and Pam had been divorced for a year and a half, but had to exchange their three children at the police department because of the intense antagonism between them. Someone had recommended that they get mediation to learn how to talk better to each other. We set up an appointment. I could not meet separately with them first, because of the distances each had to travel.

Adam and Pam both arrived in separate vehicles. When they came in, the air was absolutely icy. I went over the rules and asked if each could accept them. They said they could.

I first asked each one to tell me what their biggest issues were. I said it would be hard for the other to listen quietly, but each would have equal opportunity to listen and to speak. There were a few interruptions, which I monitored carefully.

We spent the first hour searching for a comfort zone within which we could work fairly. We spent the second hour negotiating differences and constructing an initial agreement from which to work between sessions.

Neither party was ready for the repeat and review steps, so I served as umpire. I indicated that during the next month either party could call me to report infractions of the agreement. They were not to be in contact with each other. The next meeting was set for thirty days later.

Two weeks later Adam called to report a violation of the agreement on the part of Pam. I called her to get her perspective and we agreed on a course correction.

When the time for the second session arrived, Pam was a few minutes early. We visited briefly, allowing her to share a bit more of herself with me. It was clear that she felt overpowered by Adam.

Adam was about ten minutes late. He apologized and we began to talk. When I asked each to say how the agreement had worked, each had a complaint about the other. We negotiated those complaints and made some additional course corrections to the initial agreement. They made a few brief attempts at talking to each other, but needed frequent coaching from me. The next session was set for thirty days later.

Two weeks later Pam called to report an infraction on the part of Adam. I called him to get his perspective. He tried to blame Pam for the problem and I suggested that he not escalate the tension anymore. I said we would work it out at our next meeting.

At the third session Pam was again a few minutes early. She expressed her displeasure with Adam's rudeness during the second session. When Adam arrived, I asked how things had been during the past month. This time Pam asserted herself, saying that Adam had violated his commitment. Adam tried to defend himself, but Pam did not back down. I pointed out to him that he was being a bit too forceful and rude in making his demands. He seemed taken aback, expressing that he was not aware of that. He did improve his demeanor. Soon he and Pam were talking together without my coaching assistance. At the end of the session he suggested that a fourth session might not be necessary. Pam was not so sure. We set a tentative date for forty-five days later.

Before the date for the next session arrived, Adam called and said that a fourth session would not be necessary. I asked if Pam had agreed to that and he said "Yes." He said they would call again if things got too difficult. That call never came. A year and a half later Adam called to say that they had learned how to communicate well enough to begin living together again.

Matthew 18:17

"If he refuses to listen to them, tell it to the church; and if he refuses to listen even to the church, treat him as you would a pagan or a tax collector" (Matt. 18:17).

In Jesus' day the church was patterned after the Jewish synagogue. Every small village with at least ten family heads had one and the elected elders of the village presided over it. The local rabbi participated in the discussions of that council.

When a local dispute arose between members of the village and the individuals could not work it out privately, they would take their case to the local village elders. Those elders immediately adjudicated the case.

The early house churches of the New Testament were little more than small extended families and fellowship groups. When disputes arose between Christian believers and they could not settle their differences privately, they took their disputes to the local elders of their house church, who also adjudicated for them.

How can we apply that formula to our context today? It is difficult to comprehend how an entire church of three or four hundred members (or several thousand for that matter) could reasonably mediate or adjudicate a dispute with integrity. If a smaller group of mediators cannot solve a complex issue, a large congregation would certainly be baffled. In fact, even a church of fifty members is larger than many of the churches of the New Testament era.

It seems to me that God gives an offended party three platforms on which to seek restoration of a broken relationship. The first is a private conference, the second is third-party mediation and the third is adjudication by the leaders of the church. What happens when that does not work? The Jewish leaders treated pagans and tax collectors with contempt, but Jesus ate with them and visited with them. When the time was right he answered their questions about eternal life. He defended their rights against the ruling authorities, even to his own detriment. Consequently, many of them began to follow him.

When a fellow believer refuses to be reconciled to us, it may be necessary to distance ourselves from the intimate, trusting relationship we once had with him/her. But we should not hesitate to keep in contact with him/her socially. Did a business partner embezzle funds or submit a substandard bid? You may have to end the business partnership, but you can still visit with him/her, even in jail if that is his/her sentence. Did a youth leader offend you as you were working together? You may have to stop working with the leader, but you do not have to stop being friends. The undying hope should be that someday the more intimate level of friendship you once enjoyed might return.

The following story shows how the third step of mediation can work.

Restoration to Service in the Church

One day James got a letter from the chair of his church's Board of Evangelism. It was endorsed by the entire official church board.

Several years earlier James had been the treasurer of the Board of Evangelism. During his tenure he had lost some records and a national agency was claiming that the board still owed them some money. Floyd, the current chair of the board, had contacted James several times. Whenever he asked about the missing records, James tried to evade the question. Floyd finally brought it up for discussion at a general board meeting.

During that meeting both the board president and the pastor said they would talk to James. They did, but the records still did not appear. James had just finished moving into a new home and said the boxes which contained those records were still unpacked.

Several months later Floyd brought the item up for discussion again in a general board meeting. This time he wanted the board's approval to send a letter to James demanding the records. Some thought the wording should be toned down, but they approved the letter.

The pastor stopped by James' home the next evening to prepare him for the letter. When it arrived in James' mailbox the wording was still in its original form. James' wife, Diane, was deeply offended by the letter and its tone and responded to the general board with a strongly worded letter of her own. She did inform the pastor of her intentions before mailing it. When the pastor received his copy of the letter, he called Diane to say that while he understood her pain he did not agree with the tone of the letter. Diane accepted that but did not change her position.

At the next meeting of the general board the letter came up for discussion. The pastor shared his perception concerning Diane's hurt. He referred to Matthew 5:23-24 and 18:15-17 and said that she and James would like to meet with the board at its discretion. The board set a date and Diane and James accepted the invitation.

The pastor introduced the session by referring to 2 Corinthians 5:18, Galatians 6:1 and Philippians 2:3-4. He reviewed the first three rules for fair reconciliation (report, repeat, review) and allowed Diane to speak.

Diane expressed the humiliation they had experienced at having received a letter of demand from the Evangelism chairperson. She said that a personal visit and a bit more patience would have made them feel much better about looking for the records. Several board members tried to respond to her but found the "repeat" step difficult.

James entered the conversation, stating that he recognized his failure to keep better records when he was a part of the Board of Evangelism. He apologized for that and said he would go through his boxes as soon as he could in an effort to rectify the situation, which he subsequently did. James also said he was worried about whether he would ever be able to serve the church in an elected office again. Members of the general board said they appreciated his apology. Some of them indicated that when the time was right they were sure he would be called upon to serve again. Less than a year later he was back on the slate of nominees and was elected to a different board.

These condensed narrations may sound simple to some readers, but none of them were simple to execute. In every case, people on both sides were seeing the issue through their own very different glasses. Those perceptions had to be clarified.

Also, in every case, both parties were extremely wary of the process, fearing that justice might not be done in their own personal case.

In each case the mediator had to deal with personal emotions and perceptions, as well as the emotions and perceptions of all the parties in the room.

S/he had to be careful not to let the process bog down in cycles of conversation which did not bring a solution. The mediator also had to make sure that when the meeting was over, everyone clearly understood the solutions. Signed statements were not used because the mediation was only one step in a longer process of growing and healing. Finally, there was a need for a commitment to some follow-up work so the progress made in the meeting would not be lost.

---

1. These accounts are based on actual case histories. All principle parties have given written consent to using their stories here.

CHAPTER TWELVE

Developing New Goals and Objectives Through a Planning Retreat

There are several organizational reasons why churches get themselves into conflict with pastors. One is that they do not execute clear mission statements when they call a new pastor and then issue a call on the basis of that mission statement. Organizations make the same mistake in communicating their mission statements to employees. Parents also sometimes fail to clearly inform their children of their priorities in family values and of their expectations in following household rules.

Another reason for conflict is that churches do not evaluate pastors on the basis of what the pastor's strengths are or how he could help them accomplish their mission statement. A third reason is that they do not have a clearly defined mission statement which is acceptable to the current lay leaders.

The goal of this chapter is to help a church or Christian group work through its own sense of mission in the light of its current situation. This should make it easier for the pastor and lay leaders to work together as a team, avoiding some of the difficulties that often create conflict.

A church can develop a revitalized mission statement either during the interim between each pastorate, right after the pastor comes, or at intervals of two or three years during a pastor's ministry. Such renewals are helpful because it allows groups to refocus their energies. It also helps to keep the mission statement in touch with contemporary needs.

What is a Planning Retreat?

A planning retreat is a concentrated period of time away from where you live, work and worship. It allows you to develop renewed consensus as a group and to develop new strategies for accomplishing the mission of your group. It does not have to be an expensive venture, but it is more helpful if it is

PLANNING RETREAT

WHO? All Boards and Ministry Teams of the Church!

WHAT? An event designed to set the stage for ministry in 19___ and 19___ .

WHEN? **August 9-11**
(Friday, 6:00 p.m. - Sunday noon.)

WHERE? Active Saints Retreat Center.

WHY? To agree with God and each other about ministry focus for Sept. ___ to Aug. ___ .

HOW? Bring Bibles, Notebooks, Ideas and Tennies. We'll talk and pray, laugh and play, and agree to serve God together in 19___ -19___!

COST? Paid for by the Spiritual Development Fund.

A Planning Retreat Poster

away from where the group usually functions, undistracted by schedules and telephone interruptions.

It can be held at a retreat center or campground, in a larger motel with convention accommodations, on the campus of a college, or at a larger church complex in another city.

It does not need to be a costly event, but it should be led by a person who knows how to get everyone involved in the planning process.

It does not have to develop elaborate schemes and strategies. It should help a group redefine its purpose and reenergize its spirit. It needs to contain good Bible study, good worship, good interaction and some recreation.

What Outcomes Should a Planning Retreat Produce?

1. It should produce a Purpose Statement. This overarching statement comes out of spiritual commitment to God and a study of God's book, the Bible. It answers the "Why" question. It states why the group exists and what values it holds most dear.

2. It should produce several goals statements. These statements answer the "What" question. The goals state the direction in which the church or group will move as it seeks to fulfill its purpose for being.

For example, if one part of the purpose is that people come to know God better, the goals might include such things as preaching about God, developing an evangelism program and providing for group prayer times.

3. A planning retreat should also produce a set of objectives for each goal. Objectives answer the "How" question. They provide the "nuts and bolts" information which makes it possible to actually accomplish the goals. This part of the statement includes the plans for the necessary personnel, finances, program, space and methodologies which will be used in accomplishing the goals.

Part of the objectives for the goals statement which we illustrated above might include plans for the pastor to develop a series of sermons on who God is. It might also include the development of an evangelism committee and a training program for interested people, as well as specific plans for developing group prayer times.

When Do You Need a Planning Retreat?

1. A retreat is needed when the group has lost its sense of vision and mission. It is easy to tell when that happens, because lethargy sets in and people become content to just keep the machinery running. It becomes harder to get people to volunteer for jobs in the organization and to get people to surrender sacred turf so others can participate.

Sometimes people begin wishing for a revival. Revival can come in many ways. A planning retreat can bring about revival, for the focused Bible study and warm fellowship rekindles the heart, while the solid planning for new strategies helps put the prayers into action.

2. A planning retreat can help when the mission changes, due to changes in population, congregational or constituency needs, or other factors. In our fast paced, mobile society, church populations do not always stay as stable as they used to. Old, tried and true methods do not always make sense for new populations.

How well I remember the story of the young housewife who always cut the ham hock off the ham before baking it. When someone asked her why she did so, she said that her mother taught her to do it that way. Her mother said she had been taught that way also. When the inquisitive researcher finally tracked down the grandmother she replied that *her* roaster was not big enough for the entire ham and hock to cook at the same time.

Sometimes the cutting edge of need in the church changes but the programs just keep grinding on, somewhat like the Energizer bunny. If the church really wants to minister to its current needs, it needs to reevaluate and refocus every few years to make sure it is doing what it really needs to be doing in a way that works for the present.

3. A planning retreat can also help when members of the group have different views of the group mission. People do not stay the same forever. Some seem to, but no one really does. As people change, different needs clamor for attention and different views of the church's mission surface.

This can also happen when new people are added to the church and when a new pastor comes. The genius of a planning retreat at times like this is that it gives people a chance to talk together about their needs and find renewed unity around issues with which everyone can identify.

4. Finally, a church or group needs a planning retreat when one cycle of methods and programs has run its course and the group needs to dream together again. It has often been said that the worst method anyone can use is the one they always use. It just finally wears out. No method is really bad in itself, but it can start to feel bad when people no longer respond to it, or when it no longer meets needs in the right way.

At a planning retreat people may decide to continue to address the same needs. However, they may also begin to realize that the way they have been meeting those needs is worn out and needs to be changed. As their spiritual energies are released, they have the opportunity to begin to dream new ideas and develop new plans which will meet their needs better.

At one all-church planning retreat several years ago one of the goals established was to pray more for people with special needs in the congregation. The objective for meeting that need was to set up a prayer concerns committee. Two wonderful women were selected, who actually were already keeping the informal network supplied with much of the information. But what the plan did was to incorporate some newer families into the informal network so they also became a more active part of the church.

Who Should Participate in a Planning Retreat?

As many of the persons in the group as possible should participate in a planning retreat. This could include the whole committee, the whole general board or church council, the entire ministry department, the entire church staff, or even the whole church.

A planning retreat is unique for several reasons. It gets people together in an informal setting away from where they usually meet one another. It gives them opportunities to come to know each other better. It bonds them together with love and helps them see each other's perspectives in new ways.

It also frees people to talk about their hopes and aspirations for the church or group of which they are a part. As they talk and are listened to, it strengthens their ownership of the mission of the church or group. It helps them understand better what the structures of the group are and how they work. It helps them get involved.

How to Prepare People for a Planning Retreat

1. Develop an awareness, an agreement of specific need. It is not uncommon, when new ideas are presented, for someone to say, "If it ain't broke, why fix it?"

At least two presuppositions underlie that statement. One is that the speaker is satisfied and comfortable with the way things are. To him/her, it is working just fine, thank you. There is no need to tamper with something that has worked well for him/her all these years.

The other presupposition is that the speaker is not looking at the situation from the same perspective as the one who wants to change things. Until s/he is able to see things from a different vantage point, change will never make sense.

Consequently, lots of informal conversation must precede the actual development of a planning retreat. It seldom works well to simply "report to the board" that the church needs a planning retreat. It is much better to engage in private and small group conversation for several months (or years) in such a way that the individuals of the group come to see that things are really in need of repair or updating.

Sometimes we encounter an individual in the group who has been talking about change for some time already, but no one has actually picked up on the idea. The one who wants to see a planning retreat take place can begin to support that other person's interest. S/he can also elicit consenting affirmations to the idea from others in the group. Consensus can begin to develop and the obstacle of confronting change can be overcome.

2. Assemble a planning committee that will be truly representative of the whole group. If the official board will be in retreat by itself, a committee of three individuals may suffice. If an entire department will be in retreat, a group of three to five representatives of the entire department should be involved. The same should be true if the entire church will be in retreat.

The pastor and the church moderator/chairperson or the CEO of the parachurch organization should participate in the planning process. However, it is essential for the committee to take sufficient ownership of the plans so ownership can be more easily passed along to the whole group.

3. The planning committee should be responsible for developing a program that will work for their group. This will

include timing, location, costs, retreat leaders, a group recorder and scheduling. They will also want to provide for child care, transportation for those who need assistance and cost subsidies for those unable to pay the whole cost themselves.

4. Develop consensual commitment to the planning retreat by allowing whole group input at every stage of planning. Depending upon the level of trust in the whole group, it may be wise to utilize questionnaires to allow for maximum input.

In such cases it is always important to offer several choices. The church council/general board should announce clearly that the planning committee will make all final decisions based upon the total results of information which it gathers. This procedure helps to strengthen trust and it also helps to disentangle a few from clutching power too tightly.

Questionnaires should pertain to the variables in the planning process which actually can be negotiated. They may offer preferred choices, for example, for location, dates, agenda items and type of child care. They should not include items which the pastor/moderator/CEO or planning committee is not willing to negotiate. This may include such items as speakers, leaders, inclusion of worship and recreation times and retreat format.

5. Follow-up after the retreat is essential. The planning committee should accept this as part of its assignment. Follow-up includes making sure that assignments and schedules which the group agreed to at the retreat are acted upon. It also includes helping the new task forces and committees get started in their new ministries. Finally, it must include a good plan for periodic evaluation and quality control by someone or some group of people.

Ingredients of a Successful Planning Retreat

1. Allow enough time for relaxation and processing between sessions. A retreat is a time away from work and the frustrations of daily life. It should not be crammed so full of activities and brain work that the group gets completely worn out. They should be able to look back on the retreat as a positive time for renewal and restoration of their spirits.

People who work for a living and are not in the habit of thinking theoretically or developing new strategies on a daily basis will find the brain work of a retreat taxing. No session should be longer than one-and-one-half to two hours and time for processing in between sessions should be structured into the program.

Processing does not necessarily mean free time or recreational time. It could include worship, guided conversation, or report times. There must be interaction between all the people, so the emerging goals and objectives become owned by all of them.

2. There should be enough physical space to allow for free movement, whole-group primary eye contact and small group interaction. Boxing people into a retreat center where there is no freedom of movement will tire them out and restrict the free movement of their spirits.

Seating should allow for good primary eye contact of everyone in the group. Small groups should be planned so their conversations do not distract other small groups. Child care should be far enough away so there is no distraction, but close enough so parents can easily care for emergencies.

3. A whole-group process leader is necessary to lead the planning process. It is difficult for one person to wear too many hats. If the planning retreat is designed to be a minor retooling of previously established goals and objectives, the pastor or CEO of the group can serve as that person. That is also possible if the goal of the planning retreat is primarily for the purpose of processing the pastor or CEO's agenda.

On the other hand, if the planning retreat is for the purpose of calling for new vision and new directions for the whole group, it may be appropriate to bring in an outside, neutral process leader. This individual should be one who is able to empower everyone in the group to participate. This individual should be both people oriented and task oriented and should be able to focus on helping everyone in the group accomplish the work of planning.

4. A spiritual/inspirational leader is necessary for the purpose of planning and leading worship and other spiritually uplifting moments. This person can be the pastor or CEO of the organization, or another person in the organization. It can also be an individual brought in from the outside who can offer a different perspective on God's grace and guidance.

It is probably wise for the process person and the spiritual leader to be different people. It is also helpful if at least one of them is not from the organization which is involved in the planning retreat.

5. Food, recreational activities and child care should be provided in such a way that retreat attenders are not distracted from their primary purpose for meeting. Such accommodations can be arranged easily if the retreat is held at a retreat center or motel with convention facilities. It is also sometimes possible to invite a neighboring church to provide such items for a fee.

Program Plan for a Successful Planning Retreat

You cannot judge a planning retreat to be a success until after its plans have been put into motion, people's spirits have been revived and revitalized and the new ideas have borne fruit. For that reason a planning retreat committee must plan for five things to happen.

1. One session should be devoted exclusively to a redefinition of the group's vision and perceived mission (or purpose for being). Elements which might be included in this session are a review of the history of the group, a study of biblical passages relating to the will of God for the church and elements of God's will which are appropriate to the particular church or group involved in the retreat. This should also include an increased awareness of the demographics of the group and its environment.

2. One session should be devoted to brainstorming in search of broad goal statements. These goal statements should focus on what it will take to accomplish the group mission in the group's locality and constituency at the present time.

In this brainstorming session the group should generate as many ideas as possible, without trying to prioritize or develop any of them. Goal ideas can be generated for each segment of the mission statement.

3. The planning committee should devote one entire group session to synthesizing, clarifying and prioritizing the broad target goals. It is very easy, if the brainstorming concept is followed fully, for a group of people to generate anywhere from 50 to 100 goal ideas in session two. These must be processed, synthesized and prioritized so that the best two or three in each category can filter to the top for further development.

4. Next, one or more sessions should be devoted to developing strategies (objectives) for accomplishing the goals (putting the goals into action). The planning retreat cannot end until this process begins. A lot of euphoria surrounds the process of talking about mission and goals. It is fun to talk about God's

will; it is a lot harder to spell out the details in task-oriented language so God's will actually gets done.

In order to be functional, these strategies must be specific, achievable and measurable. They must include a developmental time line, ways in which personnel will be secured, funding mechanisms, supervisory frameworks and methods for evaluation. They must be understood and owned by the whole group at the planning retreat.

Not all the details for each specific goal statement need to be spelled out at the retreat. However, the retreat should put mechanisms into place for completing the task within a reasonable period of time. There must be a definite line of supervision from the retreat task forces back to the retreat leader, pastor or CEO, or governing board, so that all the good work of the retreat does not merely end up in a file somewhere.

5. Finally, it is important to develop task forces or new committees which will implement the objectives of the planning retreat. It seldom works well to assign new tasks to old committees. If that happens, it is likely that either the new task or the old one will suffer.

The biblical principle of putting new wine into new wineskins is very apropos here. If there are not enough people to develop new committees, it might be important to reevaluate some of the previous committee assignments and tasks. Perhaps some old functions could be traded for some new ones.

The principle still pertains, however, that the group should develop new committees for new tasks. It is acceptable for some of the people on the old committee to be on the new committee. But the new committee should be allowed to organize itself in a way that works for the new task.

It is really ideal if new committees can be developed within the framework of the planning retreat structure. If that function must wait until the group gets back home, the realities of life "back on the ranch" may cause the new tasks, ideas and committees to be aborted. Besides, the people who were most enthusiastic for the new ideas should have an opportunity to participate in the new committee, or in its development.

In conclusion, remember that no plan is as good as the one everyone designed together, or as poor as the one which the group uses all the time. Therein lies the genius of a planning retreat.

A Model Planning Retreat

Before ending this chapter, we offer one model for a planning retreat which has been used successfully. For a more complete presentation see Appendix A.

Session One: Developing a Mission/Purpose Statement
Introduction and Instructions, 15-20 minutes.
- Ask each participant to speak his/her name, to test the acoustics of the room and to get people talking.
- Group singing.
- "Group Management by Objective."
- A statement of what we will do here together.
- Explanation of how the group will work in small groups.

Remembering the Past, 30 minutes.
- On the walls of this room there is newsprint (or tagboard) divided into segments of time representing eras of history in the life of this church/organization.
- Spend about twenty-five minutes moving from page to page, writing down significant things that happened in your life during each time period that you were associated with this church/group.

Small Group Bible Studies: "What is God Calling Us to Be and Do as a Group in Our Time?" 20-30 minutes.

Scripture passages which will form the central content of the Bible study:
- Acts 2:41-42 (Teaching/Fellowship/Worship/Prayer).
- John 4:19-24 (Worship).
- 2 Corinthians 5:17-21 (Reconciliation).
- Acts 17:20-23 (Unity).
- Matthew 28:16-20 (Evangelism).

(Add others as you feel God's Spirit leading.)

Each small group should pick a reporter. Then they should spend fifteen to twenty minutes *listing* (not discussing) those ideas which they believe focus on the call of God for their church/organization right now and for the next three to five years. They should return to the large group when time is called.

Report Session, 10-20 minutes.
- Each small group reporter will give a brief summary of their group's conclusions. The whole-group recorder should keep a master list of all ideas presented. Duplications are not necessarily significant at this stage of reporting.
- Allow from 30-90 minutes for a break.

Session 2: Setting Goals for the Mission/Purpose Statement
Review the Purpose Statement, 15 minutes.
- Song/Scripture and prayer.
- Synthesize the Purpose Statement into concise, one word statements for use on the summary sheets. Distribute one sheet to each participant (see Appendix A).

Brainstorming Purpose Statement Goals in Small Groups, 30-45 minutes.
- Divide into groups of six or seven in each group.
- The assignment is to think of as many ways as possible to accomplish each item of the Purpose Statement.

Report Session, 30 minutes.
- Collect all the ideas in verbal reports.
- Develop a complete list of goals for each component in the Purpose Statement.
- Allow from 30-90 minutes for a break.

Session 3: Prioritizing Goals
Review the List of Goals, 15-20 minutes.
- Song/Scripture and prayer.
- Review the list of goals for each component of the Purpose Statement to be sure it is acceptable to everyone.

Buzz Groups for Strategizing, 30-40 minutes.
- There will be one buzz group for each component of the Purpose Statement.
- People may select the one component of the purpose statement which interests them the most for this working session.
- Each working buzz group shall first prioritize the goal items pertaining to their component of the Purpose Statement.

- Then they shall spend time talking about several ways to accomplish each of the goals listed under their component of the Purpose Statement.

Report Session, 30-45 minutes.

- Distribute the sheet entitled "Our Strategies For Each Goal Include" (see Appendix A).
- Individuals may record each group's strategies for the list of goals on which they worked.
- Spend some time as a group prioritizing the components of the Purpose Statement and also the list of goals under each component of the purpose statement.

Session 4: Developing Objectives for the Major Goals

Worship and Celebration, 15 minutes.

- Sing favorite hymns/songs.
- Share favorite Scriptures and God's blessings in your life.
- Prayer time.

Review Goal Priorities and Assign Timetables, 15-30 min.

- Review the goal priorities developed in Session 3 for each component of the Purpose Statement.
- Assign tentative working timetables for each item on each list of goals.

Task Forces to Develop Objectives for High Priority Goals, 30-45 minutes.

- Use the same groups as were formed in Session 3. (People may change groups at this point if they prefer to work on a different goal.)
- Now it is time to be positive and get very specific. Do not allow discussion on more new ideas. Do not allow negative complaining about the items which are highest on the priority list.
- Answer the question, "What will we have to do (exactly and specifically) to put this goal item into effect.

Report Session, 30 minutes.

- Each group should report on its work and prepare to hand in its schedule of objective tasks for each goal to the group recorder.
- Individuals interested in helping to implement any of the specific goals may indicate their willingness to participate now or at any time after adjournment.

- If it appears that several important goals are not as fully developed as needed, plans should be made at this time to complete that task.

Closing Worship (in a way that fits your group).

CHAPTER 13

When All Else Fails

We have spent a lot of time in this book learning about conflict and how to deal with it. We first spent four chapters looking at conflict theory. The next two chapters were devoted to biblical foundations of conflict and leadership. They were followed by two more chapters which sought to provide a preliminary Christian psychological basis for understanding how conflict works. The next four chapters offered several different ways to help people overcome conflict.

But conflict does not always behave the way the books say it should. That is because people are all so very different. In many different ways they seek their own comfort above anything else. In so doing, one person or the other may become uncomfortable enough to back out of the encounter and the effort at managing the conflict "fails." At such times a conflict manager must also take care of her/himself, so s/he does not triangulate her/his own frustration.

Because no one likes to be a failure, it is almost universally true that the other party gets the blame. Obviously it is rarely true that only one party is at fault. That is so in a church/pastor conflict, a Christian supervisor/Christian employee relationship and even in a Christian family.

Sometimes the best answer is that each party's needs were so different that staying in the relationship could not bring enough contentment and comfort to make things work well enough. In such cases, parting company is not a failure; it is a better conflict management option than murder.

That leads me to suggest that this chapter could have been renamed "Before All Else Fails, What Then?" If a relational system is pushed to the extreme, one may not be able to salvage anything. In fact, once a conflict reaches the Level Three stage (see chapter three), there will be some fallout. If we learn how to recognize the early warning signs of internal turmoil, we should be wise enough to retreat from making too stringent demands, lest everything comes apart.

Too much pressure upon the psychosystem of a person or group of persons is only one reason why conflict management techniques sometimes fail. Failure may also be due to conflicting directions of the individuals within the same system.

When Growth Becomes Death

In an important book on church growth and development, Robert Dale makes the observation that there are nine normal stages in the life cycle of a church.[1]

As proposed by Dale, the nine stages in the life cycle of a church are:

1. Dream / Vision — This is the time of new church formation, when energetic and committed people band together to accomplish a specific goal for Jesus Christ.

2. Beliefs — Also known as the time of conviction/agreement, this is a time when everyone in the group is like-minded, has the same value structure and desires the same outcome.

3. Goal-setting — This stage comes quickly on the heels of vision and belief. During this time the group works together to formulate their goals for accomplishing the mission on which they agree. There is bonding, euphoria and great enthusiasm in focusing on a joint mission.

4. Structure / Organization for action — This is the time when the mission of the church can no longer be accomplished only by enthusiasm and informal networking. New members have entered the fold and structure must be added so everyone knows cognitively how the mission and goals are to be accomplished.

5. Ministry accomplishment — This stage forms the apex of efficiency, goals attainment and mission fulfillment. Everyone is participating in an organization which they designed and for which they have full ownership. They enthusiastically see new members added to the flock and slowly bring them alongside, sharing leadership and power with them.

6. Nostalgia — Now a new generation begins to take the reins of power. They make changes in the church to accommodate new people, new needs and new situations. As that happens, the older generation begins to speak in nostalgic terms of the "good old days." They long for the old hymns, the former pastor, the smallness and comfort of their earlier group and the efficient organization which they designed. They practice convenient selective memory and shift their loyalty from the

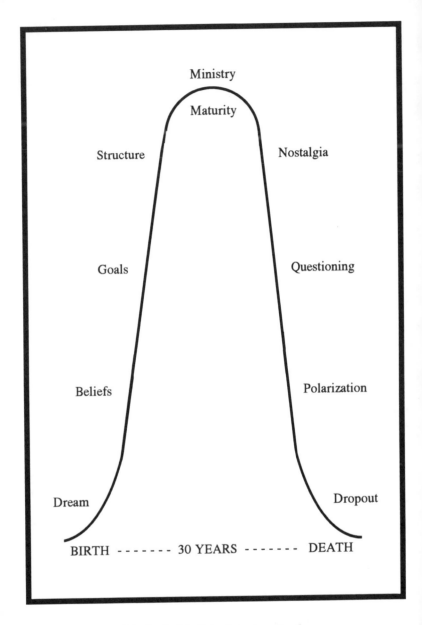

Ministry

Maturity

Structure

Nostalgia

Goals

Questioning

Beliefs

Polarization

Dream

Dropout

BIRTH - - - - - - - 30 YEARS - - - - - - - DEATH

Health Cycle Model, showing the degree of health or disease in a congregation.2

present to the past. This is the first stage of congregational disease.

7. Questioning: The point of no return — As the older group continues to long for the past, they begin, in a begrudging manner, to question the changes of the present. They refer to the way they once did things as the "right way" or the "spiritual way," and the newer ways of others as "worldly" or "liberal" or at the least as unnecessary and confusing. New pastors come with new energy and enthusiasm and innocently run headlong into nostalgic resistance.

8. Polarization: Division in the House of God — As the questioning continues, the newer leaders (often including the newer pastors) become defensive and offended. They argue in favor of their views and ways in an effort to maintain their own viability and integrity. In return, the older generation speaks out more defensively in favor of the past and the sides draw farther apart. The result is conflict, apathy and decline.

9. Dropout/Death — The final stage of the life cycle is death. In churches where people are not continually renewed in spirit by God's Spirit, organizational death eventually occurs. One by one, families and individuals relinquish ownership and commitment and either quit caring and working, or drift away to find other churches where they and their ideas are received more fully.

The Systems of a Church or Christian Group

To understand how powerful a tightly knit system or sub-system can be in a church, we might find it helpful to review the way in which Edwin H. Friedman applied systems theory to churches.[3]

Triangulation is an important aspect of systems theory and in churches the triangles are (1) my family, (2) the whole church family and (3) any individual family in the church other than mine. Comfort is defined by the way any two of these family units relate to each other. When a relationship becomes strained, one of the family units will fixate on another unit in order to seek balance. That fixation, in turn, may upset another balance and cause its own kind of friction.

When a pastoral family enters the church system, every other family unit desires to become special friends with the pastoral family. That competition strains other relationships within the church family and also puts undue stress upon the

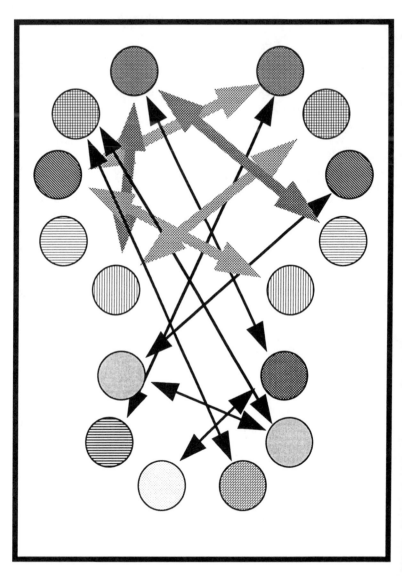

Triangulation can fragment
any happy group.

pastoral family. Efforts to find balance often produce intense moments of conflict and can bring any pastoral honeymoon period to a screeching halt.

The triangulation which a pastoral family inevitably brings to a church family is intensified by the fact that the pastor (and family) are leaders and role models in the congregation. If the pastor (and family) are too conservative or too liberal for individual families in the congregation, the latter will become uncomfortable. They will seek to set up their own triangled relationships in an effort to restrict the effect of the pastor upon their family. The pastor's family may also triangle in an effort to find stability for themselves.

To Change or Not to Change

Another key element in the complex relationship of a church is the differing abilities of persons to accommodate change. Some are comfortable with more diversity and others desire less. Invariably those families which cannot accommodate much change tend to blame the other primary relationship in the triangle and seek out the third leg of the triangle in order to stabilize themselves.

We have already observed more than once that people in churches want comfort and stability. In a time when everything else in life is up for grabs, at least they want their religious center to remain stable. The law of homeostasis (balance) states that individuals and groups of people require enough balance (status quo) in their lives to keep from losing all sense of order.

This is just as true of pastors as it is of churches. That may explain why some pastors are so quick to make changes when they arrive at a new parish. They actually desire the changes for their own peace and comfort more than for the effective work and ministry of the people they have come to serve.

A church has the right to remain status quo if that is its choice, just as much as any individual or family does. That may not seem to agree with some people's concept of evangelism, but it does agree with some other people's concept of salvation.

While some people prefer the status quo, others demand change in order to be happy. For them, it may not matter what the change is, as long as there is forward movement. They are just as discontent with sameness as their counterparts are with change. They are always looking for a new challenge, a new opportunity, a new vision. They irritate others with their constant insistence that everyone move at their faster pace.

Whether it is change or sameness, it is important to realize that churches (and pastors) always pay prices for their decisions. Stay status quo and you can expect certain outcomes. Change and you can expect other outcomes. The choice is more one of outcome than one of input. You must first decide what you want your outcome to be and then provide the input which accomplishes that goal. The right to make those choices is a part of the freedom God gives us.

Too Liberal or Too Conservative?

That brings us to another inevitable outcome of the focus of this book. We learned in chapters seven and eight of the different ways in which God created people. Sometimes we are tempted to label people as too narrow or too liberal. Actually, when we do that we make ourselves into gods. In effect we accuse God of poor design and construction. Genesis tells us that everything God made was good. That requires that we find a more positive way to think about people who are different from us.

It is, admittedly, frustrating to relate comfortably to those on the other end of the spectrum. However, the truth remains that narrowly focused individuals cannot grow easily except within their own narrow field of vision. That does not mean they are diminished as people in any sense of the term. They are just differently oriented. Some of the wisest minds have also been the most narrowly focused minds. On the other hand, those who are more narrowly focused must also learn to appreciate those whom God has created with a wider field of vision. Such persons can help others keep their balance in complex and complicated situations. We all need each other. God intended us to all live together and be friends one of another. It is a sin not to do so.

So, When All Else Fails, What Then?

How can we relate successfully to each other? Perhaps the concentric circles of communication can help us. If it is too painful to enter deeply into the lives of those who are vastly different from us, we can be content to use the exterior levels of communication to keep in touch.

We can at least learn to be civil towards and, better yet, respectful of one another and not push too hard. It is God's will. Philippians 2:4 tells us so. None of us has an edge on what is right or even what is best for the church. Only God qualifies for that. If we want to live together in God's family the way he wants us to, we have to learn to be accepting of what God says through our brother or sister, even though what they hear from God is vastly different from what we hear.

We must finally remember that our social systems, including our family, friends and church, are given to us by God to help us survive in a hostile world. That does not mean that any one person or small group of persons can hold a system hostage, anymore than any one person or small group of persons can forcibly change a system. Philippians 2:4 speaks to everyone in the system.

Mansell Pattison has written about how the intimate psychosocial network is able to help people survive in the face of immense odds.[4] Using a diagram of concentric circles, he shows the groups of persons who are vital to us in times of crisis.

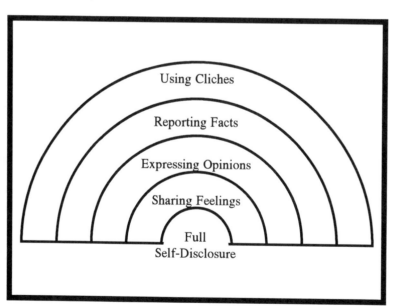

Using Cliches

Reporting Facts

Expressing Opinions

Sharing Feelings

Full
Self-Disclosure

Five Levels of Communication

Certainly the church fits into circles two, three and four. Some individuals seemingly cannot allow those circles to change too much or their entire balance in life comes apart.

Communication is an emotional phenomenon as well as an information sharing technique. People can only hear you when the relationship is right. Once you start pursuing them, forcing them to change against their will, they will shut you out. That force also is wrong. Not even God forces us to change against our will. He invites us, encourages us and even commands us, but he leaves the compliance up to us. We must bear the consequences, to be sure, but truly there is often more forcefulness between people than between God and people.

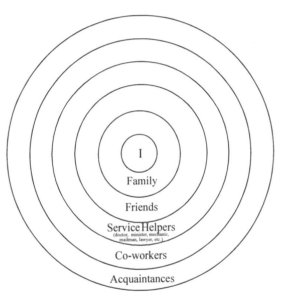

The Intimate Psychosocial Support Network

Perhaps we could learn something from the meekness of Jesus as well as from the assertiveness of Christ. It was Jesus' style to be meek as well as to confront his opponents. He did not mince words when talking to the scribes and Pharisees, but he did not win them over either. He confronted them with the truth, but they ostracized him and finally crucified him for it. In his meekness he submitted to them and in so doing won the world more quickly by his death than by his life.

Hugh Halverstadt rightly makes the point that Christian assertiveness takes into account both the rights of the other person as well as the justice of God.[5] It is right for individuals to state kindly and courteously what they believe is God's will for them. It is also right for others to state that another person's view is not God's will for them. Finally, it is right for each to agree to love and trust each other in spite of their different viewpoints. What is not right is seeking to control another person.

The final word we have to offer is that of being a permission giver. We discussed it both in chapters seven and nine. Permission giving helps us deal with people within the church system who are going in a different direction than we want to go. It also helps us deal with the many triangles which tie up our lives.

Finally, permission giving helps us relate better to people who are more conservative or more liberal than we. It helps us communicate more honestly. It helps us love more purely. It helps us forgive more genuinely. It helps us become Christian like Jesus was. That, after all, is our ultimate goal.

How we view what's important in life
determines how we make
decisions with others.

1. Robert D. Dale, *Pastoral Leadership*, Nashville: Abingdon, 1986, pp.84-91.

2. Robert D. Dale, *To Dream Again*, Nashville: Broadman Press, 1981.

3. Edwin H. Friedman, *Generation to Generation: Family Process in Church and Synagogue*, New York: Guilford Press, 1985.

4. Mansell Pattison, "Clinical Application of Social Network Theory," a special issue of *International Journal of Family Therapy*, 3 (1988).

5. Hugh F. Halverstadt, *Managing Church Conflict*, Louisville, Ky.: Westminster/John Knox Press, 1991, p. 38. See also Koch and Haugk, *Speaking the Truth in Love: How to be an Assertive Christian*, St. Louis: Stephen Ministries, 1992.

Appendix A

A MODEL PLANNING RETREAT

PERMISSION IS HEREBY GRANTED TO THE PURCHASER OF THIS BOOK TO DUPLICATE PORTIONS OF THE FOLLOWING PAGES FOR THEIR OWN USE IN DEVELOPING A PLANNING RETREAT FOR THEIR GROUP. SUCH COPIES MAY NOT BE DISTRIBUTED IN A SEMINAR OR WORKSHOP FOR WHICH A FEE IS COLLECTED, OR IN ANY OTHER SETTING DESIGNED TO CIRCUMVENT INDIVID-UAL PURCHASES OF THIS BOOK.

Session One: Developing a Mission/Purpose Statement

Physical Arrangements.
- The tables and chairs are arranged in such a way that everyone can easily see each other and the group leader.
- Provide a podium and speaker system for the group leader as needed.
- Have water pitchers and glasses available on the tables.

Introduction and Instructions, 15-20 minutes.
- Ask each participant to speak his/her name, to test the acoustics of the room and get people talking.
- Group singing.
- "Group Management by Objective."

   "Planning is a disciplined, continuous process for de-cision-making. It helps us determine the future we want to achieve; what we need to do to achieve it; how we are going to do it; when we are going to do it; how we will evaluate what happens" (Dr. Lloyd Perry).
- A statement of what we will do here together.
   * First, we will celebrate the good things God has done for the church/group in the past and clarify the call of God for our church/group today.
   * Second, we will talk together about goals which will help us fulfill the call of God as we see it for today.
   * Third, we will work on strategies by which those goals can be achieved.
   * Fourth, we will identify the objective steps which it will take to carry out those strategies.
- Explanation of how the group will work in small groups.
   * During the first two workshops the group will number off into groups of five or six.

      * During the last two workshops persons will select
        topics of interest on which to work.

Remembering the Past, 30 minutes.

- On the walls of this room is newsprint (or tagboard) divided into segments of time representing eras of history in the life of this church/organization.
- On the bottom of each sheet of paper is an identifying word for each segment of time in the history of this group (a pastor, leader, benchmark event, etc.).
- Hanging beside each strip of paper on a string is a felt-tipped marking pen.
- Spend the next twenty-five minutes moving from page to page, writing down significant things that happened in your life during each time period that you were associated with this church/group.
- When we call time, please return to your seat for the next activity.

Small Group Bible Studies: "What is God Calling Us to Be and Do as a Group in Our Time?" 20-30 minutes.

- The process of remembering what God has done in the past will likely continue throughout this planning retreat. You may continue to write things down. Remembering will also help you in your small group discussions.
- Now I want you to number off from one to "n", to form "n" groups of five each.
- Now, before you divide into your groups, I want to give all of you five Scripture passages. They will form the central content of your Bible study. If any of you want to add a passage in your small group, you may. I will also tell you how to use them in your small group Bible studies. (Do not give out the words in parentheses below.)
  - * Acts 2:41-42 (Teaching/Fellowship/
    Worship/Prayer).
  - * John 4:19-24 (Worship)
  - * 2 Corinthians 5:17-21 (Reconciliation).
  - * Acts 17:20-23 (Unity).
  - * Matthew 28:16-20 (Evangelism).

  (Add other Scriptures as you feel God's Spirit leading.)
- When you get into your small groups pick a reporter. Then spend fifteen to twenty minutes *listing* (not discussing) those ideas which you believe focus on the call of God for

our church/organization right now and for the next three to five years. Please return to your tables when we call time.

- Assign the locations of the groups and let them begin. The group process leader (you) should move around between the groups to help any that get stuck.

Report Session, 10-20 minutes.

- A whole-group recorder from within the leadership of the church/group should have been designated by the planning committee before the retreat started.
- Each small group reporter will give a brief summary of their group's conclusions. The whole-group recorder should keep a master list of all ideas presented. Duplications are not necessarily significant at this stage of reporting.
- Allow a few minutes of whole-group interaction so people can begin to reflect on what they have heard in the report session.
- Encourage people to continue the conversation about the Bible studies during the break time, but discourage negative responses such as "Yeah, but…"
- Allow from 30-90 minutes for a break.

Session 2: Setting Goals for the Mission/Purpose Statement
Review the Purpose Statement, 15 minutes.

- Song/Scripture and prayer.
- Clipped from a church bulletin:
    * "The sort of church we do not want to be is
    * a museum style church, where you go only as a spectator;
    * a hairdresser style church, where they split every hair four ways;
    * a service station style church, where you go just to be filled up;
    * a sleeping car style church, where the passengers don't want to be disturbed;
    * a refrigerator style church, where the icy chill drives out any new arrivals."
- Synthesize the Purpose Statement into concise, one-word statements for use on the summary sheets. Distribute one sheet to each participant (see page 190).

OUR *PURPOSE* FOR BEING A CHURCH IS TO:		

OUR *GOALS* FOR EACH PURPOSE INCLUDE:
1.
2.
3.
4.
5.
6.

OUR *STRATEGIES* FOR EACH GOAL INCLUDE:

1	2	3	4	5	6

Brainstorming Our Purpose Statement Goals in Small Groups, 30-45 minutes.

- Our work at this retreat is like flying in a commercial jetliner. Sometimes we fly at 35,000 feet, sometimes at 20,000 feet and other times at 10,000 feet. In order to arrive at the deplaning ramp we have to taxi in on the taxiway. In Session 1 we were at the 35,000 foot level and now we will descend to the 20,000 foot level. In each session we will descend farther, until we are on the ground again.
- Divide into groups of six or seven in each group, with a proportionate number of men and women in each group. Number the men and women from one to "n", depending upon how many groups are needed.
- Ask each group to appoint a reporter and a timekeeper.
- Instruct each group to divide their available time between all of the Purpose Statement items.
- The assignment is to think of as many ways as possible to accomplish each item of the Purpose Statement.
- This time is devoted to *brainstorming* for new goal ideas of how to *be* and *do* what God wants of us.
- Do not spend time trying to figure out how to accomplish any particular goal or how to develop any single idea. Just list as many ideas as you can.
- Do not disqualify or demean any idea at all. Every idea counts for right now. Prioritizing and fine tuning will come later.

Report Session, 30 minutes.

- Use the same whole-group recorder as before.
- Collect all the ideas in verbal reports. Combine ideas where there is duplication. (A specially designated committee may have to do some of this during the break.)
- Develop a complete list of goals for each component in the purpose statement. The group may add new ideas if any develop, but should stay on course.
- Allow from 30-90 minutes for a break.

Session 3: Prioritizing Goals

Review the List of Goals, 15-20 minutes.

- Song/Scripture and prayer.
- Thank those who have worked as reporters. Report that

there were a total of ___ different goal ideas to sift through from the last session.

- Clipped from a church bulletin:
    - * "Thank you, God, for children . . .
    - * Those sparkling eyes do not search for flaws but look for love;
    - * whose loving arms are not withheld from those who look or think differently;
    - * whose creative minds are not stifled by the desire to make more money;
    - * whose candid words do not say one thing and mean another;
    - * whose hopes and dreams are not hampered by what the neighbors may think;
    - * whose gentle kisses share the tenderness and the need for loving security."
- Review the list of goals for each component of the Purpose Statement to be sure it is acceptable to everyone.

Buzz Groups for Strategizing, 30-40 minutes.

- There will be one buzz group for each component of the Purpose Statement.
- People may select the one component of the Purpose Statement which interests them the most for this working session.
- However, each person should select a first and a second choice.
- There should be not less than three and not more than ten persons in each working group.
- Each group should first select a reporter. This reporter shall be prepared to make a verbal report to the whole group and shall also submit their handwritten notes to the whole-group reporter for reference purposes.
- Each working buzz group shall first prioritize the goal items pertaining to their component of the Purpose Statement.
- Then they shall spend time talking about several ways to accomplish each of the goals listed under their component of the Purpose Statement.
- Do not worry about developing the specific steps necessary for implementation. That will come in Session 4.

Report Session, 30-45 minutes.
- • Use the same group recorder as before.
- • Distribute the sheet entitled "Our Strategies for Each Goal Include" (see page 196).
- • Individuals may record each group's strategies for the list of goals on which they worked.
- • Allow each buzz group to report on the strategies which they developed for their list of goals. It is acceptable if the time limit did not allow them to work on each goal.
- • Spend some time as a group prioritizing the components of the Purpose Statement and also the list of goals under each component of the Purpose Statement.
- • By this time enthusiasm will have started to build to make commitments to various individual goals. Announce that in Session 4 opportunity will be given to make such commitments as desired.

Session 4: Developing Objectives for the Major Goals
Worship and Celebration, 15 minutes.
- • Sing favorite hymns/songs.
- • Sharing of favorite Scriptures and God's blessings.
- • Prayer time.

Review Goal Priorities and Assign Timetables, 15-30 min.
- • Clipped from a church bulletin:
   "Life spends itself.
   Life cannot be banked.
   Life cannot be stored for a rainy day.
   Life cannot be tucked inside a mattress.
   Life cannot be hid under a basket.
   Life cannot be buried.
   Life is sacrificial.
   Jesus spent his life, so we have it."
- • Review the goal priorities developed in Session 3 for each component of the Purpose Statement.
- • Assign tentative working timetables for each item on each list of goals, including when each item should begin, when it should conclude (if there is a conclusion time) and how and by whom it should be evaluated.

Task Forces to Develop Objectives for High Priority Goals, 30-45 minutes.
- • Use the same groups as were formed in Session 3. (People

may change groups at this point if they prefer to work on a different goal.)

- Each group should begin working on the highest priority goal in their component of the Purpose Statement. It is not essential that work on the goals must be completed. It is better to develop one or two good goal strategies than to talk superficially about many.
- Now it is time to be positive and get very specific. Do not allow discussion on more new ideas. Do not allow negative complaining about the items which are highest on the priority list.
- Answer the media reporter's questions: Who, What, When, Where and How.
- Answer the question, "What will we have to do (exactly and specifically) to put this goal item into effect?"
- Get down to the "nuts and bolts" of planning.

Report Session, 30 minutes.

- Each group should report on its work up to this point and prepare to hand in its schedule of objective tasks for each goal to the whole-group recorder.
- Individuals in the whole group may make suggestions for purposes of refinement and coordination with the objectives of other goals. It is not necessary to get bogged down in long discussions here. Those persons responsible for supervising the implementation of the entire planning retreat will care for those details.
- Individuals interested in helping to implement any of the specific goals may indicate their willingness now or at any time after adjournment.
- If it is possible to form new ad hoc committees, this is the time to do it.
- If it appears that several important goals are not as fully developed as needed, plans should be made at this time to complete that task.
    * It may be done after a break.
    * It could be done within a week or ten days of returning home.
    * It could also be done by those individuals responsible for coordinating the results of the planning retreat. (However, this is the weakest plan for this

group will be busy enough with their continuing primary assignment.)

Closing Worship (in a way that fits your group).

- This time may include Communion.
- This time may include a commitment service.
- This time may conclude with a group prayer written for the occasion.
- This time may conclude with Revelation 5:12, "Worthy is the Lamb who was slain, to receive power and wealth and wisdom and strength and honor and glory and praise."

Appendix B

STUDY GUIDE QUESTIONS

Chapter One: *Resolving Disputes in Christian Groups: An Introduction*

1. Read James 4:1-3 aloud in class. Brainstorm answers to the following questions and write them on the white board or on newsprint taped to the wall.
    a. Which desires within you cause fights and quarrels among you?
    b. What are the wrong motives we use asking for things that are not good for us?
2. List your own definitions of conflict on the white board or on newsprint. Compare them with the definition on page 5 of this book. What insights can you glean?
3. Read James 4:7-10 aloud in class. How can you reduce conflict in your life?
    a. What does "submit to God" mean? According to James 4:1-3 how can we submit?
    b. What are the ten action words (verbs) in this text which can help reduce conflict in your life?
4. Why are we tempted to avoid talking about conflict (see p. 5)?
5. Which definition of conflict do you like the most, the English definition or the Chinese definition? What do you think of the author's definition which brings the two definitions together?
6. If 5% of a group are innovators, 15% are early adapters, 60% are status quo, 15% are late adapters and 5% are against all change, what does that mean for your family, church, or Christian group?
7. On a scale of 1% to 100% how much of each type of conflict is found in your life?
    a. Ordinary daily disagreements.
    b. Sharp disagreements which cause hurt feelings and negative conversation.
    c. Such deep disagreements that a relationship is threatened.

8. Use the same scale to rate how often each type of conflict occurs in your life.
    a. Personal values which are attacked or threatened.
    b. Goals in your life which help you enjoy life according to your values.
    c. Methods (ways) by which you choose to live your life in all its details.
9. Use the same scale to rate how often you use the three major conflict management styles.
    a. Competing with others (I win, you lose).
    b. Accommodating others (I give in, you win).
    c. Collaboration with others so the problem gets solved (I win and you win).
10. As you conclude this lesson write out a short prayer based on James 4:1-3,7-10. Let it contain a thought or a feeling which God has given to you in this study.

Chapter Two: *How Can Good People Do Bad Things to Each Other?*

1. Review briefly your understanding of conflict. Brainstorm brief one-line definitions of conflict and place them on the white board.
2. List the causes of conflict which are given on page 17 of the text. Which of these causes rank highest in the experience of your family or group?
3. List the four major physical functions, or "early warning signs," which accelerate when tension begins to develop within a person.
    a. Which is the first one you notice within yourself?
    b. What other physical functions may accelerate in your body when tension begins to develop?
    c. What is the best way to manage our emotions when these functions accelerate?
4. Another way to define role dilemma is to ask the question, "Who's . . .?"
    a. Is that question usually spoken out loud in the midst of a debate or does it behave as a quiet, annoying, unspoken fear?
    b. How can we tell when a conflict has shifted

from tension development to role dilemma? (Glean the answer from the narrative of Pastor Bob and the church board.)

    c. What is the most effective way to deal with the role dilemma stage of the conflict cycle?

5. Make a list of the injustices which people tend to collect when they move into the third stage of a conflict cycle.

    a. How effective are these injustices in solving the problem?

    b. What happens to relationships when these injustices are used?

    c. What is the right way to resolve a conflict when it reaches this stage of the conflict cycle?

6. In what ways does "war" occur when the conflict moves into stage four in a Christian group or family?

    a. Think of some of the "wars" you have been involved in. Did it move towards a good solution for everyone?

    b. What brought the confrontation to an end?

    c. In what way would you have liked it to end?

    d. Does a "war" ever end fairly for everyone?

7. After a confrontation is over, how do adjustments take place?

    a. List the choices each individual must make.

    b. Which of those choices do you normally prefer? Why?

8. After one conflict is resolved, what can you expect concerning future conflicts?

    a. In what ways can you use conflict to help you in the future?

    b. What can we learn from Paul's experience with conflict?

Chapter Three: *The Five Deepening Levels of Conflict*

1. Have four persons read aloud 1 Samuel 9:18-10:1, 13:5-14, 15:1-29, and 28:1-20. On the white board label each narrative in the following manner:

    a. 9:18-10:1, A Problem to Solve: Israel Wanted a King.

    b. 13:5-14, A Very Unfortunate Moment: Saul Needed a Sacrifice **Now**!

    c. 15:1-29, A Clear Contest: Who Was Really in Charge in Israel?

    d. 28:1-20, Too Late to Change Things Now: Saul Had His Chance.

2. Conflict Level One: Discuss the first biblical narrative briefly.

    a. What was the problem that needed solving?

    b. Was there total agreement about the solution?

    c. How did total agreement come about (10:17-25)?

3. What are the four rules for keeping a Level One conflict from escalating into a Level Two conflict?

    a. What is the difference between reporting, and accusing or demanding?

    b. Why is it important to repeat back to the other what s/he has just said? Take time to practice the report/repeat routine several times in class.

    c. Explain the value of reviewing all the options. How does a group develop several options?

    d. What is the value of periodic reevaluation of the choices you have made earlier? How can you keep it from becoming "personal?"

4. Conflict Level Two: Discuss the second biblical narrative briefly.

    a. In what way did Saul experience discomfort?

    b. In what way did Samuel experience discomfort?

    c. How did ego protection make it impossible for either Saul or Samuel to remain cordial to each other?

    d. Whom do you suppose became the supporters of Saul's viewpoint? Of Samuel's viewpoint?

5. Pretend that your group or class was living in Saul and Samuel's time, and became concerned about restoring unity between the two. Mention several strategies you could have developed, based on the discussion in this chapter.

6. Conflict Level Three: Discuss briefly the third biblical narrative.

    a. In what ways did this episode become a contest between opposing sides? What issues were at stake? Why could neither side afford to give in?

b. Mention some of the distortions that occurred in this narrative.

c. What are some of the steps necessary for resolving a Level Three conflict? How could some of these steps have been implemented in this biblical narrative?

7. On the white board, list several Level Three conflicts between people of which you are aware. (Be careful not to reveal confidences.) How could these conflict resolution strategies resolve the contemporary conflicts which you know about?

8. Conflict Level Four.

a. What elements of a Level Four conflict do you see in the 1 Samuel 15 narrative?

b. How often does a Level Three conflict slide easily into a Level Four conflict?

c. What is really at issue in a Level Three/Level Four conflict?

d. What is the best way to resolve a Level Four conflict? What made it impossible for the 1 Samuel 15 conflict to be resolved?

e. Who are some qualified people whom you know that could resolve a Level Four conflict in your life?

9. Conflict Level Five: Discuss briefly the fourth biblical narrative presented in today's lesson.

a. Which elements made it impossible to resolve the break in relationship between Samuel and Saul in this narrative?

b. What immediate outcome of a Level Five conflict did Saul experience in this narrative? What ultimate outcome did he experience (chap. 31)?

10. What strategies for dealing with a Level Five conflict did Samuel employ?

a. For what reasons was it impossible for Samuel to perform an intervention and place Saul under discipline to restore his spirit?

b. How quickly (or slowly) should an erring Christian be placed under discipline when s/he is involved in a conflict?

c. What are the dangers of placing a believer under

discipline too soon, too late, or in the wrong manner?

d. What biblical precedents do we have for acting decisively in the life of an erring believer? In what manner should we act?

e. What does 2 Corinthians 2 teach us about concluding an act of discipline?

Chapter Four: *Five Conflict Management Styles*

1. On the white board make a list of the ways people in the class handle their conflicts. Allow each one to use whatever terminology comes to their mind.
2. Avoidance.
    a. Poll the class. When conflict occurs, how many of them seek to avoid it at all costs? How many prefer to confront it?
    b. List some illustrations of avoidance in the Bible. Was avoidance the right choice to make in those instances?
    c. List some examples of avoidance in the lives of class members. Was it the right approach for them to take? Why/why not?
3. Accommodation.
    a. List some illustrations of accommodation in the Bible. Would you have responded in a different way?
    b. What does accommodation say to the person? What are some of the blessings of accommodation? Some of the dangers?
4. Competition.
    a. Is competition always bad? What are its weaknesses and its strengths?
    b. When is competition the right approach to take?
    c. What three emotions can trigger a competitive approach to conflict?
    d. When does competition become a sin?
5. Compromise.
    a. What are the two risks in compromise? Are they bad, good or neutral?
    b. What does a compromising approach say to the other party?

c. List some examples of compromise in the Bible. Were they the right approach? Why or why not?

   d. Aside from the moral issues, what are the dangers and the blessings of compromise?
6. Collaboration.
   a. Give a good definition of collaboration.

   b. What does collaboration do for all the parties in a conflict?

   c. What makes it hard to collaborate?

   d. List some biblical examples of collaboration.
7. In what ways can spiritual discipline help us manage our conflicts better?
8. What is the difference between being aggressive, submissive, and assertive?
9. When is power useful? When is it dangerous?
10. What rule must people with more energy and drive follow to equalize the power of those who move more slowly and gently?

Chapter Five: *A Biblical Theology of Conflict Management*

1. Review the five biblical principles of conflict management.
   a. Discuss the statement "conflict is a reality in all of life."
      i) How does that make class members feel?

      ii) What does it make them think about?

      iii) Why does the text say that God placed enmity between humankind and Satan?

      iv) Discuss some of the Scriptures given for the first principle.
   b. Why is the best rule for dealing with conflict "adopting the mind of Christ?"
      i) What does it mean to adopt the mind of Christ?

      ii) How can we do that?
   c. Why is it important to **put forth** personal efforts to make peace?
      i) How can we best live in harmony with others?

   ii) What great lesson does Philippians 2:3-4 teach us about peacemaking?

   iii) What is the key to using Matthew 18:15-20 in the right way?

2. Read 1 Corinthians 10:1-13 in class.

  a. What is the one great teaching of this text?

  b. How can it apply to managing conflicts?

3. On the white board provide three columns. Above the first write "conflict management style," above the second write "positive outcome," and above the third write "negative outcome." Then fill in the numbers as you proceed through this study.

4. Avoidance.

  a. How many negative and positive occurrences of avoidance are found in the Bible?

  b. What types of corresponding conflicts might occur today that would fit into the three categories in the Scriptures?

5. Accommodation.

  a. How many negative and positive occurrences of accommodation are found in the Bible?

  b. Study the positive examples given in the text. What are some ways accommodation could be used today to further the work of God?

  c. What dangers of accommodation must we guard against (both moral and psychological)?

6. Competition.

  a. How many negative and positive occurrences of competition are found in the Bible?

  b. When is competition wrong and when is it right today?

  c. When we must "compete," what rules should we follow?

  d. Why are we so quick to compete with others, and how can we manage it better?

7. Compromise.

  a. How many negative and positive occurrences of compromise are found in the Bible?

  b. What can we learn about the rightness and wrongness of compromise from studying the two examples given in our text?

8. Collaboration.

a. How many negative and positive occurrences of collaboration are found in the Bible?

b. When collaboration fails, as it did three times in the Bible, does that mean it was wrong to try?

9. Study the chart in the text or on the white board. What lesson can we learn about using the five styles?

10. What three approaches to conflict management receive strong theological support in the Scriptures?

Chapter Six: *Profiles of Problem Solving in the Early Church*

1. Divide the white board into four columns. Label the columns "Name," "Leadership Style," "Positive Traits," and "Negative Traits."

   a. Place the names of Moses, Joshua, Samuel, David, Early Church, and Paul in the first column.

   b. Opposite each name, in the second column, write the words prophetic, charismatic, collaborative, autocratic, eldership, and supervisory.

2. Review the story of Moses briefly, as given in the text. List the positive and negative traits of the prophetic leadership style.

3. Review the story of Joshua briefly, as given in the text. List the positive and negative traits of the charismatic leadership style.

4. Review the story of Samuel briefly, as given in the text. List the positive and negative traits of the collaborative leadership style.

5. Review the story of Saul and David briefly, as given in the text. List the positive and negative traits of the autocratic leadership style.

6. Review the story of the early church briefly, as given in the text. List the positive and negative traits of the eldership leadership style.

7. Review the story of the apostle Paul briefly, as given in the text. List the positive and negative traits of the supervisory leadership style.

8. Which leadership style/s does your class prefer?

9. Select one narrative or incident from that leadership style given in the biblical text.

   a. Answer the Who, What, Where, When, and

How questions for that narrative. Be as specific as you can.
    b. What good things were taking place?
    c. What problems/challenges were the principle parties of the passage facing?
    d. Would another leadership style have made a difference in the outcome of the situation? Explain.
10. Is one leadership style appropriate for every type of group or situation? Explain.
11. What conclusions about biblical leadership styles can you draw from this study?
12. Preparation for next chapter's study: ask for volunteers who will give a brief two or three minute synopsis of each of the subtopics on pages 70-82 of the text.

Chapter Seven: *Personality Clashes and Forgiveness*

1. Begin the class by reading Jeremiah 17:9 and Matthew 18:21-22.
2. Place on the white board the headings "Personality Differences," "Emotional Pain," and "Issues of Power."
    a. Under each heading list the subheadings of each section.
    b. Ask those who volunteered at the end of the last session to present their reports. Allow for brief questions, if there are any.
3. Discuss the question: In the light of so many personality differences, from a Christian viewpoint is it right or wrong to engage in negative conflict with another person?
    a. What shall believers do when one person is con-vinced that s/he is right because God has revealed the truth to him/her?
    b. What conflict management style is appropriate when a group of believers has strongly held different points of view on any matter?
4. When there are different points of view or it is time to make a change, what four biblical principles can help make the process more godly?
    a. Permission-giving.

i) Who is the greatest permission giver of all time?

  ii) What are the benefits of permission giving?

  iii) How are the six principles of permission giving biblically based?

b. Reframing the interests.

  i) Is it always possible to look at a problem from a different angle?

  ii) After everyone has stated their view of the problem, what is the next question to ask?

c. Forgiveness.

  i) In what way is forgiveness a two-way street?

  ii) What three steps must take place for forgiveness to bring reconciliation?

d. Assertive caring.

  i) What is the difference between assertive and aggressive or passive communication?

  ii) How can the five rules for assertive communication develop better communication and behavior?

Chapter Eight: *Managing Your Emotions in a Conflict*

1. Begin the class by reading Psalm 139:1, 13-14 and 1 Thessalonians 5:23.

2. Discuss the statement "The bottom line in all conflict is individual discomfort." Do you agree or disagree? Can you give illustrations to support your view?

3. Divide the white board into three columns. Label the first "Biblical Teaching," the second "Protective Feelings," and the third "Pleasant Feelings (Shalom)." Under the column heading "Protective Feelings," place the three words "sad," "startle," and "anger." Under the column heading "Pleasant Feelings (Shalom)," place the three words "happy," "excited," and "tender."

4. Assign six people to read the one paragraph definition of each of the six basic feelings on pages 110-12. After reading each definition, turn to the following section in the text and complete the columns entitled "Biblical Teachings" for the three protective feelings.

5. Discuss the section in the text entitled "Four Early Warning Signs."

    a. What early warning signs are you aware of first?

    b. What other early warning signs, not listed here, do you experience? Can they be tied to one of the four basic ones?

    c. What can we do when we become aware of an early warning sign so that we do not behave wrongly? How can we manage the intensity of our intense emotion at that moment?

6. How does the section entitled "Comfort Zones" help you answer question 5c above?

7. Discuss the section entitled "Surprises at Metropolitan Avenue." Be sure to give everyone a chance to speak. Divide into small discussion groups if possible. What positive lessons can you learn from this discussion?

8. As you end the class reread Psalm 139:1, 13-14 and 1 Thessalonians 5:23. What new insights have you gained today about these two important biblical statements?

Chapter Nine: *Conflict Management Tools for Servant Leaders*

1. Read Matthew 20:25-28 together in class.

    a. Does "servant" in this passage imply giving up your own views? Explain.

    b. Which of the five conflict management styles is required if your group wishes to follow this scriptural teaching? Talk about how that might work in your own situation.

2. What is the difference between authoritarian rule and authoritative rule?

3. What is the underlying biblical principle relative to making decisions by consensus?

    a. Determining who is in charge, or

    b. determining that all are equals facing a problem to solve?

4. In what important way or ways do the six principles for successful living given on pages 102-3 make it possible to fulfil the Scripture passage you are studying today?

5. What important hermeneutical principle must we remember when applying early church New Testament principles to our church situation today?

6. In what four important ways is active listening different from passive listening and disinterested listening? How does active listening work in the church? In the family? In Christian organizations?
7. In perceptions clarification, what/whose perceptions need to be clarified?
8. What four points are important in order to clarify perceptions adequately? Can you think of additional points?
9. How can you go about the task of teaching people to develop better relationships?
10. When working with conflict resolution, what does empowerment mean? What four rules are important for accomplishing this goal?
11. What is the final obstacle to overcome in dealing with conflict? How does our scripture help us accomplish that?
12. Note: Make assignments today for the role play which is planned for the next lesson. Encourage people to read over their own part carefully so they will be comfortable with it.

Chapter Ten: *Conflict Management in a Committee Meeting: A Role Play*

1. Follow the instructions for the Role Play in chapter ten of the book.
2. During the last ten minutes of the class period, make a list of Scripture passages on the white board which can help to guide you in your future participation in committee meetings.

Chapter Eleven: *The Fine Art of Mediation: Three Case Studies*

1. Read Matthew 5:23-24 and 18:15-17 at the beginning of the class session. On the white board write out the questions:

   a. Who is responsible for mediation of a dispute?

   b. What are the three stages of resolving a dispute?
2. According to the text, what is the most significant personal element in mediating a dispute? Do you agree or disagree? Why?

3. Matthew 18:15. What are the four steps in mediating a dispute? If you wish, role play the four steps in class several times.
4. Matthew 18:16. What is the purpose of the two or three witnesses? How should they be chosen?
5. Discuss the ground rules for a third-party mediation. How well would they work in a family mediation?
6. Matthew 18:17. In the phrase "tell it to the church," who or what is the church? What is the purpose in telling it to the church?
7. How does Matthew 18:17b-20 help provide for a fair, honest Christian response to unrepentant wrongdoing?
8. How important is follow-up after a mediation session is completed?

Chapter Twelve: *Developing New Goals and Objectives Through a Planning Retreat*

1. What are three reasons that churches and Christian groups get themselves into trouble with conflict?
2. Scan through the following headings in chapter twelve, and discuss those elements of the chapter which fit your situation.
    a. What is a planning retreat?
    b. Of what does a planning retreat consist?
    c. When do you need a planning retreat?
    d. Who should participate in a planning retreat?
    e. How to prepare the people for a planning retreat.
    f. Ingredients of a successful planning retreat.
3. What are the current goals and objectives of your study group, or the group to which you belong which is the object of this study?
4. In what ways could a planning retreat improve the function of your church or group?
5. If your class feels the need for a planning retreat (for themselves, their church, or their group) what steps could you take to implement such an endeavor?
6. Spend time listing incidents in the Bible where planning was evident. In what ways did the planning improve the event? In what ways could the planning have been better?

7. In what ways does a "planning retreat" benefit your personal life?

Chapter Thirteen: *When All Else Fails*

1. List on the white board several failed encounters and enterprises in the scriptures. Do not overlook David and Saul, and Jesus and Judas Iscariot.
2. Why do you think this chapter is titled the way it is?
3. Review the nine stages in a life cycle of a church (or group). In which stage do you think your church or group is? Why?
4. What are some of the "triangles" which you think exist in your church or group? Are they healthy or hurtful? What can you do about it?
5. When is change good? When is it bad? When should you accommodate those who cannot tolerate change? When you cannot accommodate them, how can you make changes in a more Christian manner?
6. What do you think about the liberal/conservative debate in our country? What solution to the polarization is there for Christians?
7. Review the last section of the chapter. When you have done everything you can to bring about change and/or heal wounded spirits and it does not come out perfectly, what can you do next?
8. Take some time to discuss those elements of this book that have already made an impact in your life and in the lives of those close to you. Affirm members of your class or group in whom you can see positive changes. Pray for those who desire greater growth and change in their own lives.
9. What elements of conflict management must you still work on? List them on the white board.
10. Read together James 4:1-3, 7-10. Close with prayers of thanksgiving to God for new growth in your life and with prayers of rededication for those elements that still trouble you.

Appendix C

ORDER FORM FOR MBTI SERVICES

Many families and Christian groups can improve their communication and interpersonal relationships by understanding basic differences in the way they make decisions and live their lives.

If you are interested in enriching your life in this way, clip (or photocopy) the form below and mail with a check or money order in U.S. funds to:

Resources for Resolving Life's Issues
2123 Wold Avenue
P.O. Box 9673
Colorado Springs, CO 80932-0673
U.S.A

For information on MBTI Seminars, Teamwork Building Consultations, Family Communication and Sensitivity Workshops and Church Leadership or Conflict Reduction Consultations, write to the above address or contact:

1-719-380-1065   1-800-477-3007
FAX 1-719-544-7885

Office Hours: 8:30—4:30, Mountain Time, Monday through Friday, except holidays

Amount	Item	Price	TOTAL
	MBTI Self Scorable plus		
	interpretation	25.00	
	MMTIC (for children) plus		
	interpretation	25.00	
	Introduction to Type	3.50	
	A Parent's Guide to Type	5.00	
	A Teacher's Guide to Type	5.00	
	God's Gifted People	6.00	
	Please Understand Me	12.00	

SUBTOTAL	
Tax (if applicable)	
Shipping (10% for books ordered)	
TOTAL	
…Check …Money Order	

…Visa/MasterCard #:	Expiry Date
NAME	DATE
SHIPPING ADDRESS	
CITY/STATE/ZIP	

BIBLIOGRAPHY

Blackburn, Richard. *How Do I Manage Differences*. Lombard, Ill.: Lombard Mennonite Peace Center, 1989.

Carlson, David E. *Counseling and Self-Esteem*. in Collins, Gary R., gen. ed., Resources for Christian Counseling. Waco, Tex.: Word Books, 1988.

Claassen, Willard. *Learning to Lead*. Scottdale, Penn.: Herald Press, 1963.

Classen, Ron and Riemer, Dalton. *Conflict and Peacemaking in Churches*. Fresno, Ca.: Center for Conflict Studies and Peacemaking, Fresno Pacific College, 1991.

Cruse and Cruse. *Understanding Co-dependency*. Deerfield Beach, Fla.: Health Communications, 1990.

Dale, Robert D. *Pastoral Leadership*. Nashville: Abingdon, 1986.

Dale, _____. *To Dream Again*. Nashville: Broadman Press, 1981.

Dow, Ron et. al. *Training Course on Utilizing Conflict in the Church*. Topeka, Kans.: Congregational Development Committee, Christian Church in Kansas, 1991.

Fairfield, James G.T. *When You Don't Agree: A Guide to Resolving Marriage and Family Conflicts*. Scottdale, Penn.: Herald Press, 1977.

Foster, Richard J. *Celebration of Discipline: The Paths to Spiritual Growth*. San Francisco: Harper & Row, 1978.

Friedman, Edwin H. *Generation to Generation: Family Process in Church and Synagogue*. New York: Guilford Press, 1985.

Friedman, Meyer and Ulmer, Diane. *Treating Type A Behavior--and Your Heart*. New York: Alfred A. Knopf, 1984.

Halverstadt, Hugh F. *Managing Church Conflict*. Louisville: Westminster/John Knox Press, 1991.

Haugk, Kenneth C. *Antagonists in the Church: How to Identify and Deal with Destructive Conflict*. Minneapolis: Augsburg, 1988.

Henfelt, Minirth and Meier. *Love is a Choice: Recovery for Codependent Relationships*. Nashville: Thomas Nelson, 1989.

Hollinger, Ellen, ed. *Crossing the Boundary: Professional Sexual Abuse Educational Packet*. Akron, Penn.: Mennonite Central Committee, 1991.

Hurd, Pattison and Llamas. "Models of Social Network Intervention," *International Journal of Family Therapy*, 3(1981):4:246-57.

Keirsey, David and Bates, Marilyn. *Please Understand Me: Character and Temperament Types.* Costa Mesa, Ca.: Matrix Books, 1978.

Keleman, Stanley. *Emotional Anatomy: The Structure of Experience.* Berkeley: Center Press, 1985.

Koch, Ruth and Haugk, Kenneth. *Speaking the Truth in Love: How to be an Assertive Christian.* St Louis: Stephen Ministries, 1992.

LaHaye, Tim. *Spirit-Controlled Temperament.* Wheaton, Ill.: Tyndale House, 1966.

Leas, Speed B. *Discover Your Conflict Management Style.* Washington, D.C.: Alban Institute, 1984.

Leas, _____. *Moving Your Church Through Conflict.* Washington, D.C.: Alban Institute, 1985.

Lebacqz, Karen and Barton, Ronald G. *Sex in the Parish.* Louisville: Westminster/John Knox Press, 1991.

Littauer, Florence. *Personality Plus: How to Understand Others By Understanding Yourself.* Tarrytown, NY: Fleming H. Revell, 1983.

Mains, David. *Healing the Dysfunctional Church Family.* Wheaton, Ill.: Victor Books, 1992.

Marston, William M. *Emotions of Normal People.* New York: Harcourt Brace, 1928.

McBirnie, William Steuart. *The Search for the Twelve Apostles.* Wheaton, Ill.: Tyndale House, 1973.

McCaulley, Macdaid and Kainz. "Estimated Frequencies of the MBTI Types," *Journal of Psychological Type IX*(1985):3-9.

Morris, Dixie and Frank. *Therapeutic Feelings: A Companion for Adventurers.* Arlington Heights, Ill.: Liberation Psychology Training Center, 1988.

Myers, Isabel Briggs. Gifts Differing. Palo Alto, Ca.: Consulting Psychologists Press, 1980.

Oswald, Roy. *Power Analysis of a Congregation.* Washington, D.C.: Alban Institute, 1980.

Pattison, Mansell. "Clinical Application of Social Network Theory," a special issue of *Internatinal Journal of Family Therapy,* 3 (1988).

Peck, M. Scott. *People of the Lie.* New York: Simon and Schuster, 1983.

Perkins, Bill. *Fatal Attractions: Overcoming Our Secret Addictions.* Eugene, Ore.: Harvest House, 1991.

Perry, Lloyd M. *Getting the Church on Target*. Chicago: Moody Press, 1977.

Qualben, James. *Peace in the Parish*. San Antonio: Langmarc, 1991.

Richards, Lawrence O. *A New Face for the Church*. Grand Rapids: Zondervan, 1970.

Riordan, James. "Six Blind Men and an Elephant," *An Illustrated Treasury of Fairy and Folk Tales*. Twickenham: Hamlyn, 1986.

Sell, Charles. Unfinished Business: *Helping Adult Children Resolve Their Past*. Portland, Ore.: Multnomah Press, 1989.

Shawchuck, Norman. *How to Manage Conflict in the Church*, 2 vols. Irvine, Ca.: Spiritual Growth Resources, 1983.

Springle, Pat. *Rapha's 12-Step Program for Overcoming Codependency*. Houston: Rapha Publishing/Word, 1990.

Strauch, Alexander. Biblical Eldership: *An Urgent Call to Restore Biblical Church Leadership*, 2nd ed. Littleton, Colo.: Lewis and Roth, 1988.

Strayhorn, Joseph M., Jr. *Talking It Out: A Guide to Effective Communication and Problem Solving*. Champaign, Ill.: Research Press, 1977.

Swets, Paul W. T*he Art of Talking So That People Will Listen*. New York: Prentice Hall, 1983.

Thomas, K.W. and Kilmann, R.H. *Thomas-Kilmann Conflict Mode Instrument*. Tuxedo, NY: Xicom, 1974.

Thomas, Marlin E. *A Study of Conflict in the Bible*. Colorado Springs, Colo.: Resources for Resolving Life's Issues, 1988.

Thomas, _____. "The Pastor's Role in Managing Church Conflict," *Direction*, 19:2(Fall 1990):65-74.

Thomas, _____. "8 Reasons Why Pastors Cross the Boundaries of Sexual Propriety," *The Christian Leader* (Oct. 8, 1991): 5-6.

Voges, Ken and Braund, Ron. *Understanding How Others Misunderstand You*. Chicago: Moody Press, 1990.

Wiebe, Katie Funk. "Sex in the Workplace," *The Marketplace*. (Nov/Dec, 1989), 4-9.

INDEX